365 outdoor activities you have to try!

Jamie Ambrose

LONDON, NEW YORK, MELBOURNE,
MUNICH, AND DELHI

DK LONDON
Project Art Editor Clare Joyce
Project Editors Wendy Horobin,
Ruth O'Rourke Jones, David Summers
Editor Lili Bryant
Senior Preproduction Producer Ben Marcus
Senior Producer Alice Sykes
Jacket Designer Mark Cavanagh
Jacket Editor Manisha Majithia
Jacket Design Development Manager Sophia MTT
Managing Art Editor Michelle Baxter
Managing Editor Angeles Gavira Guerrero
Publisher Sarah Larter
Associate Publishing Director Liz Wheeler
Art Director Philip Ormerod
Publishing Director Jonathan Metcalf

DK INDIA
Managing Art Editor Sudakshina Basu
Managing Editor Rohan Sinha
Senior Art Editor Mahua Sharma
Art Editors Kanika Mittal,
Shreya Anand Virmani
Editor Suefa Lee
DTP Designers Neeraj Bhatia,
Syed Mohammed Farhan, Bimlesh Tiwari
Preproduction Manager Balwant Singh
Production Manager Pankaj Sharma

First published in Great Britain in 2014 by
Dorling Kindersley Limited
80 Strand, London WC2R 0RL

This edition produced for
The Book People Ltd, Hall Wood Avenue, Haydock,
St Helen's, WA11 9UL

2 4 6 8 10 9 7 5 3
008 – 192378 – Mar/2014

A CIP catalogue record for this book
is available from the British Library

ISBN 978-1-4093-4951-8

Printed and bound by Leo Paper Products, China

Discover more at **www.dk.com**

BE SAFE! IMPORTANT NOTE TO PARENTS

Some of the activities in this book require adult supervision. Always ensure that your child follows instructions carefully and remember to keep them safe when exploring outside. The Publisher has set out some basic guidelines on safety see pp.4-5, but it is the responsibility of every user of this book to assess individual circumstances and potential dangers of any activity they wish to undertake. The Publisher cannot accept any liability for injury, loss, or damage to any user or property following suggestions in this book.

The Publisher would draw the reader's attention to the following particular points:

- Plants may be poisonous or protected by law from picking or uprooting
- Fungi and berries should only be collected for consumption at reader's own risk since many fungi and some berries are poisonous
- Wild animals may bite or sting – take suitable precautions and a first aid kit

Contents

How to use this book

This book is full of fun and exciting things to do, from building a den to pressing flowers and trapping bugs. Take it with you wherever you go and you'll find an activity that helps you explore the natural world. It doesn't matter if the book gathers a little dirt along the way – just don't let it gather dust on your shelf.

Photographs and clear step-by-step instructions show you what to do at each stage

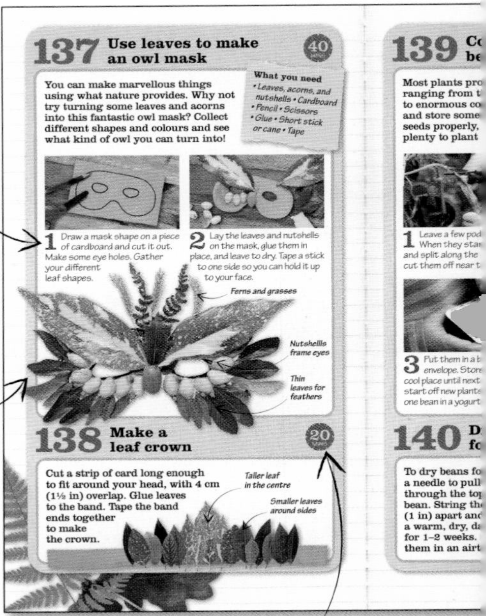

Larger pictures show you what your finished projects should look like, so that you can copy them

A clock symbol shows you how long you'll spend doing an activity. This does not include any downtime, such as waiting for things to grow or dry out.

rspb giving nature a home

The RSPB works for a healthy environment rich in birds and wildlife. The RSPB is the UK's largest nature conservation charity, inspiring everyone to give nature a home.

Wildlife Explorers is the junior membership of the RSPB. To find out more and how to become a member visit **www.rspb.org.uk/youth**

If you would like to know more about the RSPB, visit: **www.rspb.org.uk** or write to: RSPB, The Lodge, Sandy, Bedfordshire SG19 2DL. Tel. 01767 680551

Children – be safe!
Tell an adult before you do any of the activities in this book as you will need an adult to supervise these activities.

Pay attention to this symbol: it means you need to take extra care with some parts of the activity. Follow the instructions carefully.

Follow the countryside code when you are out and about:

- **Plan ahead, be safe, and follow any signs**
- **Leave gates and property exactly as you found them**
- **Protect plants and animals and take your litter home**
- **Keep dogs on a lead**
- **Consider other people**

And remember – you should release any animals you investigate back into the wild (preferably in the place you found them) at the end of an activity.

A "What you need" checklist shows you the equipment you should have ready before you start the activity and the items you will need to collect

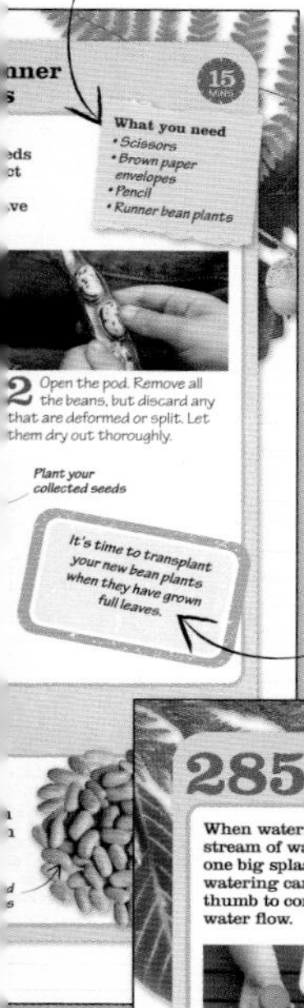

Information stamps include top tips to help you complete the projects (green), fun facts (blue), safety tips (pink), and suggestions of alternative things to try (orange)

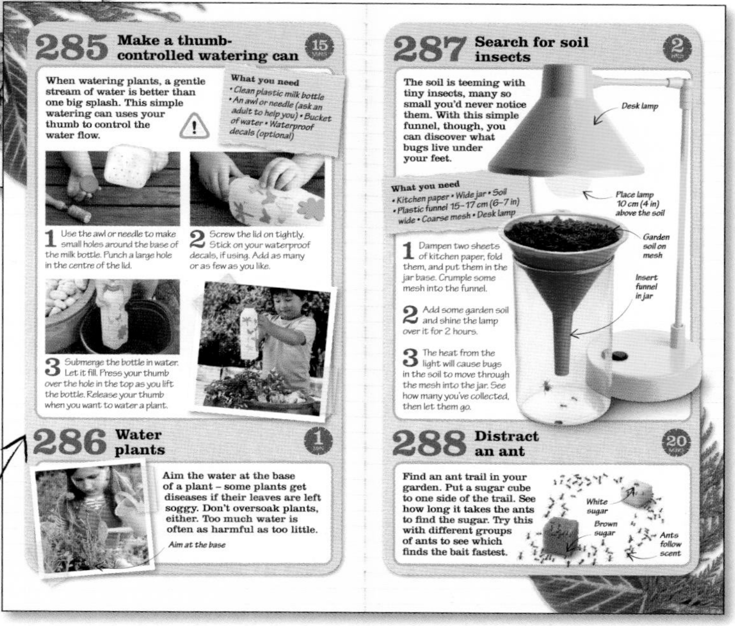

Activity number – each activity is numbered so you can keep track of what you have done – there's an activity number for every day of the year!

001 Make a seed box

1 HR

Gather and store seeds to grow your favourite garden plants the following year – for free. Collect them when the seed pods are ripe, dry them, and store them in this box. Keep it in a cool, dry place until spring.

What you need
• Shoebox, with lid • Wrapping paper • Tape • Scissors • Cardboard • Paint, marker pens • Small brown envelopes

1 Wrap the box and lid in wrapping paper. Cut dividers from the cardboard the same width as the box. Paint or mark them in seasonal designs.

2 Decorate the envelopes. You could draw the plant whose seed you'll put in each envelope. Put your seeds inside.

3 Seal the envelopes. Label each with the seed name and date of collection. Put each in the right section and close the lid.

002 Fly a seed helicopter

2 MINS

Some trees, such as maple, have winged seeds to travel on the wind. If you find one, hold it by the round part of the wing, throw it straight up in the air, and watch it spin like a helicopter.

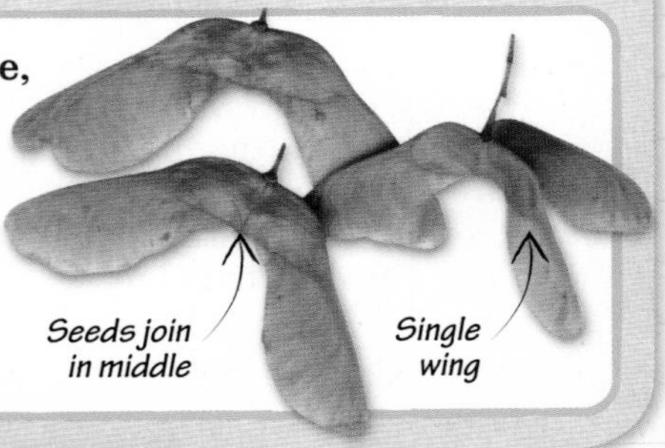

003 Make a bumblebee nest box

20 MINS

Bumblebees nest in the ground. The queen bumblebee usually tries to find an abandoned mouse or vole hole by tracking the scent of the rodent's nest, but you can help out the bees by building this bumblebee nest box.

What you need

- Trowel
- 4 stones
- Flowerpot
- 12 x 12 cm (5 x 5 in) piece of slate
- Hay or wood shavings

1 Dig a hole in the ground deep enough to hold the flowerpot. The pot needs to be ceramic, with a central drainage hole.

2 Drop in some hay or wood shavings. This will help the queen to find it as it smells like a mouse's nest.

3 Put the upturned flowerpot in the hole, set out the stones in a square shape around it and place the slate on top to keep out the rain.

004 Plant a bee-friendly garden

15 MINS

Fill your garden with flowering bee-friendly plants such as lavender, buddleias, anemones – anything with nectar-rich flowers. Species that bloom at different times will give bees a constant food source.

005 Build a den

40 MINS

Set up a den near a tree in the garden and you'll have your own private hideout, a place to hang out with your friends – or spend the night in if you make it waterproof enough and the weather's fine.

What you need
• Canes or poles • Material: tarpaulins, sacking, old bedding are ideal • Twine or rope • Big tree

1 First decide where you want your den to be. Building it next to a large tree not only gives you an instant "back wall", it also provides cover, shade, and extra stability if the den leans against it or is tied to its trunk or branches.

Waterproof groundsheet

2 For a simple framework, arrange the canes in a teepee. Push the bottom ends into the ground, then tie them together at the top with twine.

3 Drape and tie on your fabric pieces to the canes. You might use all non-waterproof material first, then cover them with a tarpaulin if you want to use the den in wet weather.

4 If the ground is damp, lay a waterproof groundsheet or tarp down as a floor. Remember to leave an opening for a doorway!

006 Make a slingshot catapult

5 MINS

Stretch a thick rubber band across a strong, forked stick. Insert a paper ball or dried pea between your thumb and finger and pull back the rubber band. Aim at a can or rock (never animals or people), and let fly.

007 Thread a flower garland

40 MINS

Fresh flowers are nature's perfect decorating tool. Why not show them off to fantastic effect by making this flower garland? It's ideal for a summer garden party or barbecue.

!

What you need
- Fresh flowers: chrysanthemums or marigolds are ideal
- Thin garden wire
- Scissors

1 Snap or cut off the flowers just below the head. Cut a 70 cm (2½ ft) length of wire and twist a loop at one end.

2 Push the unlooped end of wire into the centre of the stem and up through the flower. Slide the flower along.

3 Add flowers until the wire is nearly full. Finish with another loop. Make more strands in the same way. Use the loops to hang your garlands up.

008 Hang a flower curtain

1 HR

Instead of making curvy swags with your garlands, leave them as long strings. Hang the garlands vertically next to each other from a branch to make a magical flowery curtain.

Add ribbons if you like

009 Plant a round pizza garden

45 MINS

You can't grow cheese, pepperoni, or dough, but you can grow many of the plants used as pizza toppings. Plant your favourites in a round container, and add dividers to make a living "pizza".

What you need
• Scissors • 6 foam pizza bases • Waterproof paint • Trowel • Circular container • Compost • Pizza plants: basil, tomatoes, oregano, peppers, garlic, onions

1 Paint the pizza bases. You could label them with the names of your pizza plants.

2 Put some rocks into the container for drainage, then fill it with compost. Push in the dividers to make "slices".

3 Add your plants, filling in any gaps with more compost. Water them well, and again whenever the soil looks dry.

010 Grow your own herbs

20 MINS

Choose seeds of your five favourite herbs, such as sage, parsley, dill, basil, and thyme. Sow parsley in an "X" to divide the container into four, then sow the other herbs, one per section. Water well.

011 Build a butterfly bar

45 MINS

Butterflies feed at flowers, sucking up nectar with a long, tube-like structure called a proboscis. Tempt them in with this butterfly bar full of sugary treats.

What you need
- Ripe banana
- Mixing bowl
- String
- Saucepan
- Wooden spoon
- 100 g (3½ oz) dark brown sugar
- 250 ml (8¾ oz) water
- Paper plate

1 Ask an adult to help you with the first two steps. Peel the banana and slice it into a bowl. Mash it up with the fork.

2 Put the banana, sugar, and water into a pan and gently simmer. When it becomes sticky, but is still a bit runny, turn off the heat and let it cool.

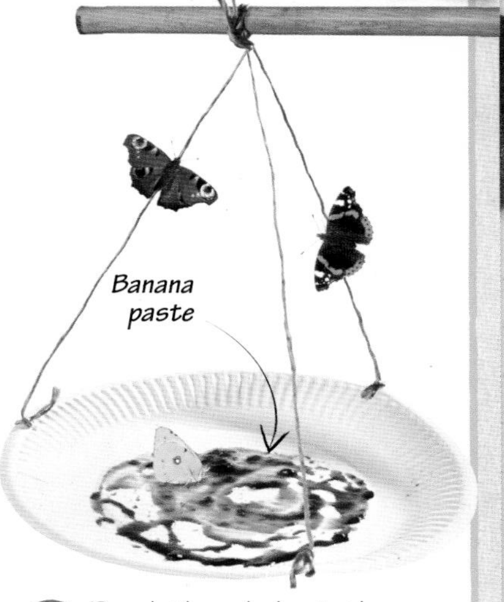

Banana paste

3 Punch three holes in the paper plate, thread a piece of string through each one, and tie with a knot. Hang the plate on a branch, spoon on some paste, and wait for butterflies to land.

012 Attract butterflies

30 MINS

Tempt butterflies into your garden by planting their favourite flowers. Buddleia is so popular that it's even called the "butterfly bush". Daisies and lavenders are also good choices.

Butterfly feeding at a clover flower

013 Keep a nature-day photo journal

1 DAY

What you need
- *Nature journal or notebook*
- *Pen or pencil*
- *Digital camera*

Next time you visit your favourite natural place, why not make a photo journal of the experience? Whether it's a woodland, a beach, or your local park, taking pictures will help you remember it – and enjoy it later, too.

My house

1 Start by noting down where you are in your journal, then take a wide shot of the environment, showing landmarks or notable features in the background.

2 Next, focus on the details. If you find a favourite wild flower or insect, take a photo. Look up, look down, and everywhere in between.

3 If you find something you can't identify, note down where it is – shade, sun, sandy soil, rich earth – in your journal. Then between your notes and the photo record you may be able to identify it when you get home.

Bee on scabious flower

014 Make a nature photo postcard

10 MINS

Take a digital photo of a friend or family member – or get them to take one of you – enjoying the natural world. Print it, write it, and send it "snail mail" or use it as an e-postcard.

A day among the wild flowers

015 Build a birdbath

20 MINS

You may already be helping birds by putting out food, but they also need water to survive. Why not make them this birdbath so they have somewhere to drink and to keep their feathers clean?

What you need
- *Shallow bowl*
- *Small stones, pebbles, and shells, rinsed*
- *Clean plastic bottle and cap*
- *Drawing pin*
- *String*

1 Put small stones in the bottom of the bowl. Set it on a tree stump near bushes or trees. Add slightly larger pebbles or shells.

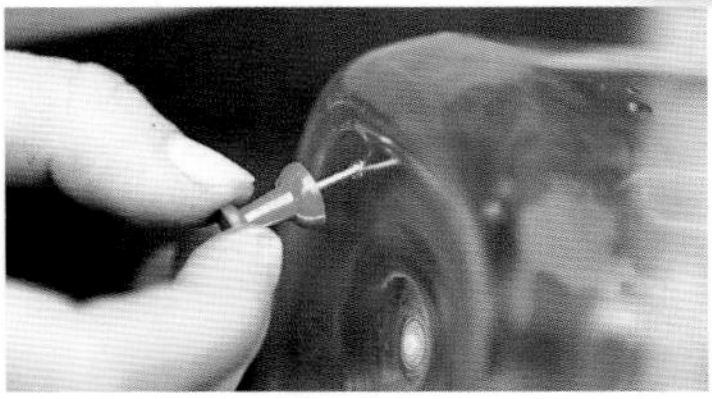

2 Make some holes in the bottle base. Fill the bottle with water, screw on the cap, attach the string, and hang it over the bath.

3 Add some water to the bowl. Clean it out every few weeks with mild disinfectant to remove any bacterial growth.

016 Turn a dustbin lid into a birdbath

10 MINS

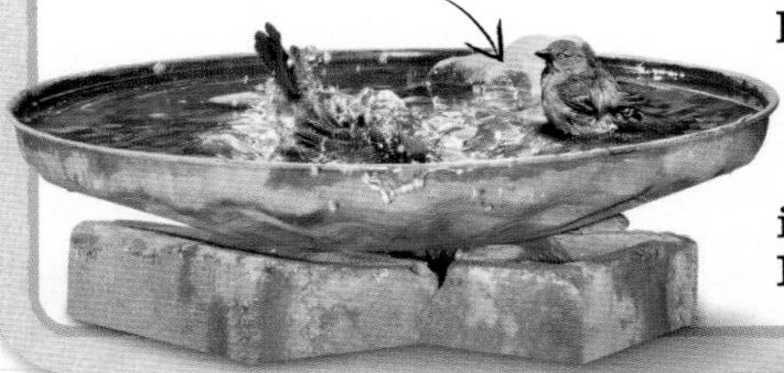

Set three bricks in a triangle on open, level ground. Put the upturned lid on the bricks. Add a layer of pebbles, especially in the deepest part. Fill with water.

017 Make a potted gift kit

20 MINS

Next time you need a gift for someone special, why not put together this flowerpot kit? Not only will the lucky person be able to enjoy the flowers far longer than cut ones, he or she will have the pleasure of planting them too!

What you need
- Flowerpot and drip tray
- Flower seeds
- Ribbon
- A small bag each of gravel and compost

1 Fill two plastic bags – a small one with gravel and a larger one with compost. Tie these with cheery ribbons.

2 Put the bags and seed packet inside the pot and put the drip tray on top to make a lid.

3 Cut two long lengths of ribbon and lay them out in a cross. Put the pot on top. Tie one ribbon around it first, then tie the other. Bring the ends all together in a bow.

018 Give a scented posy

10 MINS

Find the most fragrant, sweet-smelling flowers in your garden, such as lavender, roses, and jasmine. Arrange them in a bouquet, tie them with a pretty ribbon, and then give them to someone as a present.

019 Make a daisy chain

10 MINS

What you need
- *Lots of daisies*

If you have daisies growing in the lawn, then you have everything you need to make a daisy chain. Once you've got the hang of it, why not see how many different things you can make?

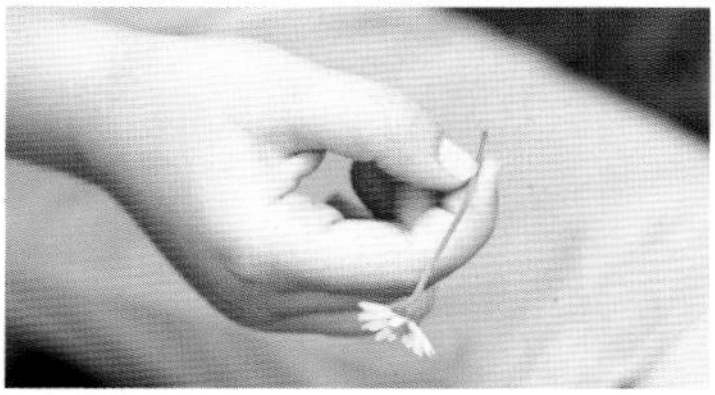

1 Pick a few daisies with long stalks. Use your thumbnail to split the stalk of one near the bottom of the stem.

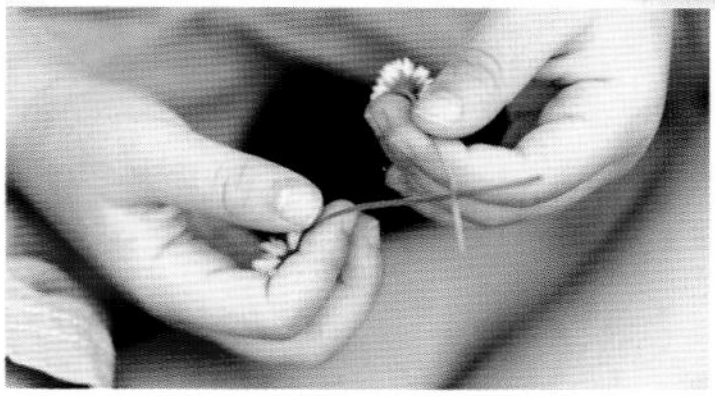

2 Thread another daisy through that hole, then make a split in the second daisy's stalk and thread a daisy through that.

3 Keep going until you have a really long chain. Make a garland or crown by carefully threading the first flowerhead through the last split stem.

020 Blow a dandelion clock

1 MIN

Try to blow them all at once

Find a dandelion seed head and try to blow all the seeds away. According to folklore, the number of puffs it takes will tell you the time – so three puffs is 3 o'clock.

021 Look for space rocks

20 MINS

Every day, about 500 tonnes of rock from space collides with our planet. Most burn up as shooting stars, but tiny particles often float to Earth. Try this experiment and you may find some of these micrometeorites.

What you need
- *Magnet*
- *Paper cup*
- *String*
- *Sheet of white paper*
- *Magnifying glass*
- *Tweezers*

1 Tie a loop of string to the cup as shown. Put a strong magnet inside. Take this outside and tap it gently on dry ground.

2 When black specks show on the cup base, take it indoors. Put it on the white paper. Take out the magnet. Tap the cup to release the specks.

3 Use a magnifying glass and tweezers to pick out rounded specks. These could be magnetic iron or nickel micrometeorites.

022 Make a Martian landscape

15 MINS

Put some sand in an old tray. Snip bits of wire wool over it. Moisten the sand with salty water and leave for a few days. As the wire rusts, the sand turns red, like that on Mars.

023 Make a fossil mud pie

2 HRS

Professional fossil hunters spend weeks slowly removing layers of soil from fossils so that they stay intact. Do you have what it takes to be a true fossil hunter? Make a fossil mud pie, swap it with a friend's, and find out!

What you need
- Objects to bury
- Garden soil
- Spade
- Bucket
- Mug
- Trowel
- Water
- Old mixing bowl or large plastic container
- Paintbrush
- Tweezers

Brush gently

Slowly reveal your fossil

1 Collect some bones or shells, or manmade items like coins to bury. Put three spadefuls of soil in a bucket. Break it up with a spade, then crumble it with your hands. Remove twigs, stones, or other rubbish.

2 Add six mugfuls of soil to the bowl. Add half a mugful of water and mix into very thick mud with your hands. Add more water if needed to make a thick, but not runny, mud that will set well.

3 Bury your objects inside the mud. Leave the bowl to set in a dry place. Swap your bowl with a friend and start to excavate!

4 Carefully remove the soil with the trowel, working from the outside in. Brush away loose soil. Lift fragile objects with tweezers.

024 Hunt for fossils

20 MINS

You can find fossils anywhere – even in the gravel in your drive. Look for them in stones, on beaches, chalk cliffs, limestone hills, or riverbanks.

Ammonites

025 Press flowers

30 MINS

If you have masses of flowers in the garden, why not preserve some by pressing them? It's easy to do, and once dried, you can use them to make bookmarks, pictures, gift tags, greeting cards, and more.

What you need
- Flowers and leaves
- Heavy books
- White blotting paper
- Scissors

1 Open a heavy book. Cut a piece of blotting paper about the same size as the open book, fold it in half, then open it again.

2 Lay the paper across the book. Arrange the flowers on the right half, with plenty of space between each.

3 Carefully fold the left side of the paper over the flowers. Close the book over the blotting paper. Put more books on top. Leave to dry for at least four weeks.

026 Dry and press seaweed

30 MINS

Rinse the seaweed and arrange it on a piece of paper. Set this on newspaper. Put waxed paper on top, wax-side down. Add newspaper, then heavy books. Change the newspaper daily. In 10 days, the seaweed will be dry.

027 Make a butterfly painting

10 MINS

The wings of a butterfly are usually mirror-images of each other. By painting on one side of a piece of card and folding it over, you can mimic this effect with a colourful outcome.

What you need
- *A sheet of card*
- *Poster paint*
- *Paintbrush*
- *Pens, pencils, or crayons*

1 Fold the piece of card in half. Paint a design on one side – you can just blob paint around. Be sure to put some along the fold.

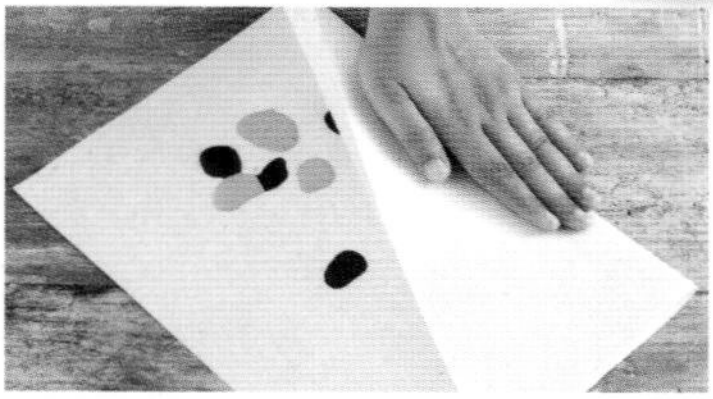

2 Fold the card in half and press down, rubbing from the centre outwards. Unfold your painting and let it dry.

3 Your painting should now be almost identical on both sides of the paper. If you like, use pens, pencils, or crayons to add legs, antennae, or even a face to your "butterfly".

028 Damselfly or dragonfly?

3 MINS

Dragonflies are much larger than their damselfly relatives. Watch the insect land – if it keeps its wings unfolded at rest, it's a dragonfly. Damselflies keep theirs folded up.

029 Make a bug hotel

1 HR

Insects need shelter in the winter – somewhere safe, warm, and dry. Recycle scrap wood and natural items into a bug hotel. In spring the bugs will repay you by pollinating your plants.

What you need

• Fir cones • Teasel heads • Drilled wood blocks • Canes • Dry branches • Stems • Wooden frame

1 Ask an adult to help you use some scrap wood, such as pallets, to construct a frame for your hotel. Ours is a big rectangle, but yours can be any size or shape.

2 Insert stems, canes, fir cones, drilled blocks of wood – any items that fit and contain crawl spaces for insects.

3 Pick a site for your hotel. Make sure it's in a sheltered location, facing southeast or southwest, if at all possible.

4 Hang it on a wall, or put it next to one at ground level. Cover all the compartments with wire mesh for more stability if you like.

030 Investigate a tree gall

15 MINS

Galls are growths on leaves, branches, and bark caused by insects, viruses, and fungi. If you see one on a leaf or acorn, carefully cut it open – you could find a developing insect inside.

This oak apple gall is caused by a wasp

031 Carve a Halloween jack-o'-lantern

45 MINS

Jack-o'-lanterns have been made for centuries at Halloween, supposedly to ward off evil spirits. Today we carve them for fun. See what kind of face you can create on your pumpkin!

What you need
- Ripe, round pumpkin
- Pencil or pen
- Knife • Metal spoon
- Old newspaper
- Bowl • Tealight

1 Spread out a thick layer of newspaper. Ask an adult to cut around the top of the pumpkin. Remove the lid.

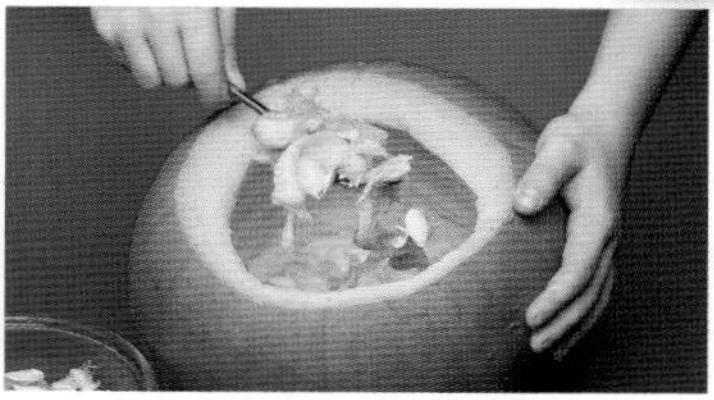

2 Scoop out the flesh and seeds into a bowl. You could save the seeds to toast and eat.

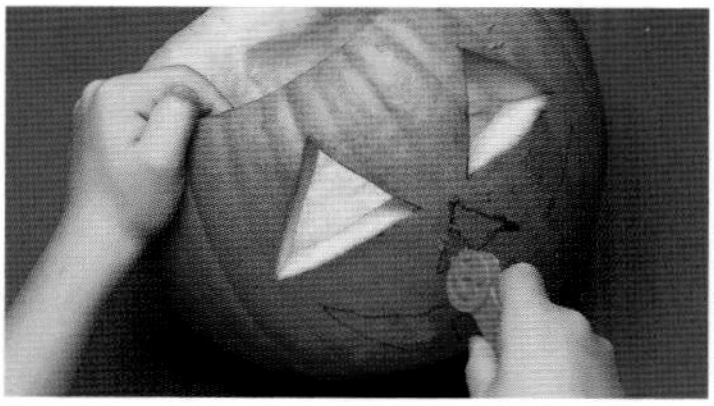

3 Draw on a face – triangles are easy to do – then get an adult to cut the pieces out. When you're finished, put a tealight inside and let it shine.

Try different shapes for eyes

032 Hang a pumpkin lantern

10 MINS

Make hanging lanterns out of small pumpkins or squashes. Cut designs in the same way as for the jack-o'-lantern, but make a hole in each side so that cord can be tied on for hanging.

DIAMONDS

FACE LANTERN

NIGHT SKY

033 Make a parachute

25 MINS

Make this great parachute with a scrap of cloth, a cup, and thread. Launch it by throwing it straight up into the air. Add a small piece of clay to the cup as a weight and see if it affects how it falls.

What you need

- *Round piece of material 30 cm (12 in) in diameter*
- *Darning needle*
- *Paper cup* • *Thread*

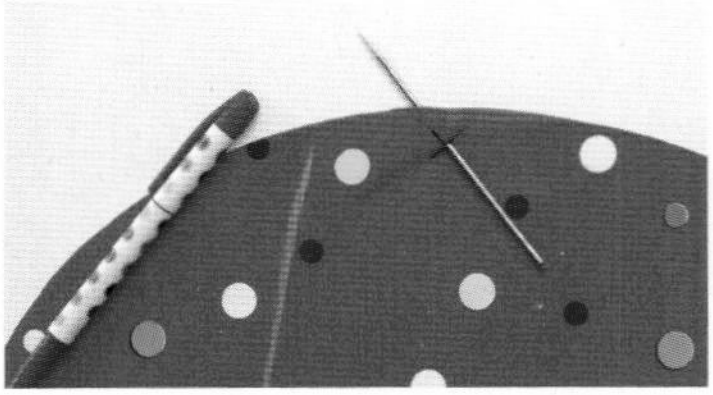

1 Make four holes in the edges of the cloth equal distances apart, like the four points of the compass.

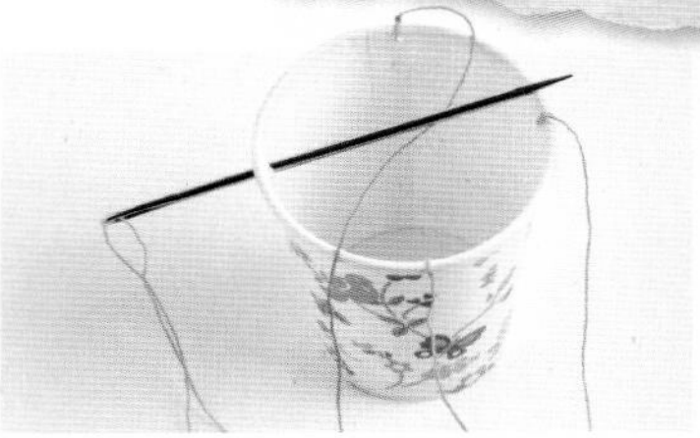

2 Use the needle to push four 30 cm (12 in) threads through four equally spaced holes in the cup's rim, and tie to the cup.

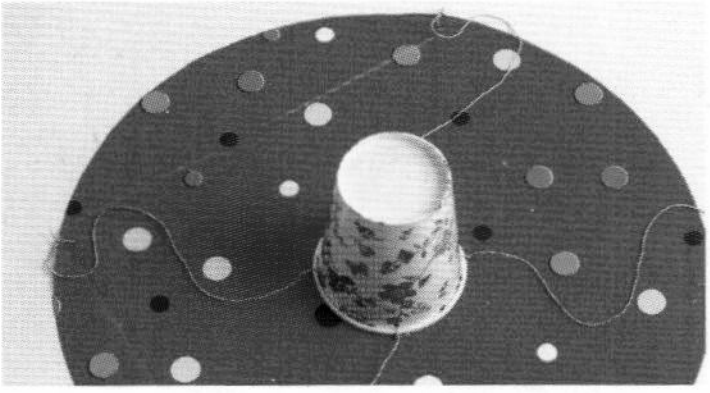

3 Put the cup upside-down in the centre of the cloth. Use the needle to pull each thread through one of the cloth holes and secure with a knot.

Try it with and without a weight

034 Throw autumn leaves in the air

15 MINS

Throw autumn leaves into the air. How many can you catch as they fall? Which shapes fall slower than others? Spray-paint a leaf, put it in the pile, then see who can find it fastest when you throw them.

035 Lay an insect pitfall trap

15 MINS

What you need
- Trowel
- Yogurt pot
- Bait (cheese, fruit, meat)
- 4 stones
- Tile or piece of wood 10 cm (4 in) square

While humans sleep, many insects are on the move – flying through the night air or crawling over soil. Make a pitfall trap and catch some of these nocturnal creepy-crawlies. Just be sure to let them go again.

1 Dig a hole in soft ground and bury the pot so that its rim is level with the soil. Pack soil around the pot edges. Drop in some bait.

2 Put the stones on the ground around the trap and place the tile on top to make a rainproof roof.

3 Leave the trap overnight. Dig up the trap to view your catch. Note down what you've caught, and try again.

036 Lift logs to find insects

5 MINS

Lift a log to see underneath. Ants, beetles, woodlice, and centipedes may be living there. Put the log back safely.

037 Make a kite

1 HR

Flying a kite is one of the best ways to have fun in the summer. You just need a field, a park, or anywhere that's free of trees and overhanging wires. Add a breeze and your kite, and you're ready for take-off.

What you need
- Split canes or basketweaving reeds
- Glue • Tissue paper
- Cotton thread
- Stapler • Kite string

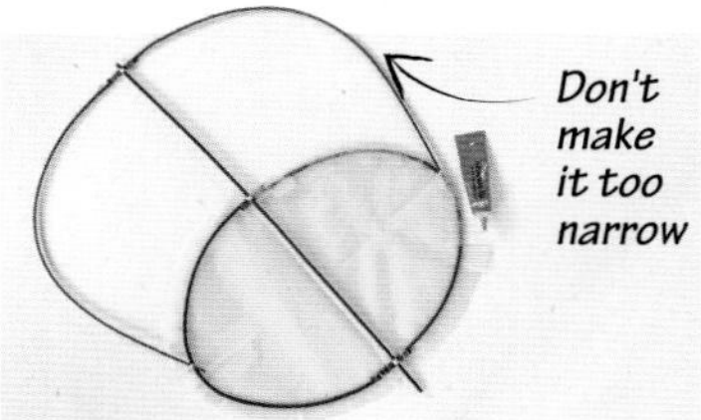

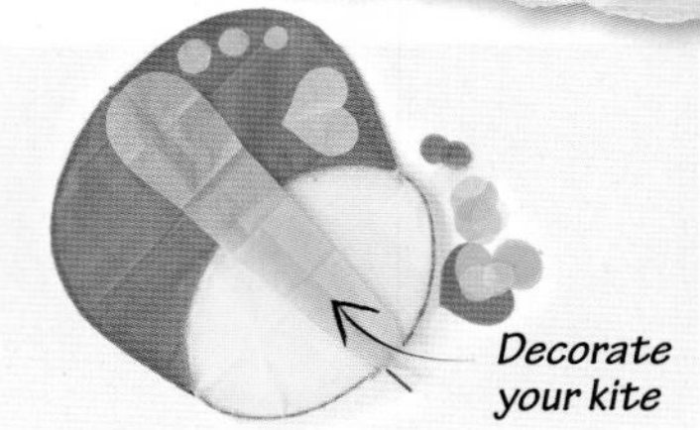

1 Soak the canes overnight. Tie them together in a frame. Put glue on the bottom half and lay the frame glue-side down on tissue.

2 Cut around the frame leaving a 5 cm (2 in) border. Snip the border, fold it over, and glue down. Repeat with the other half.

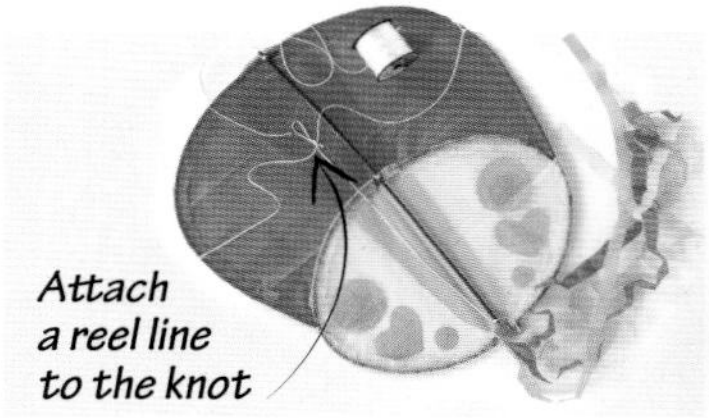

3 Cut two pieces of string, one slightly longer and the other wider than the kite. Knot them together in the middle then tie the ends to the frame.

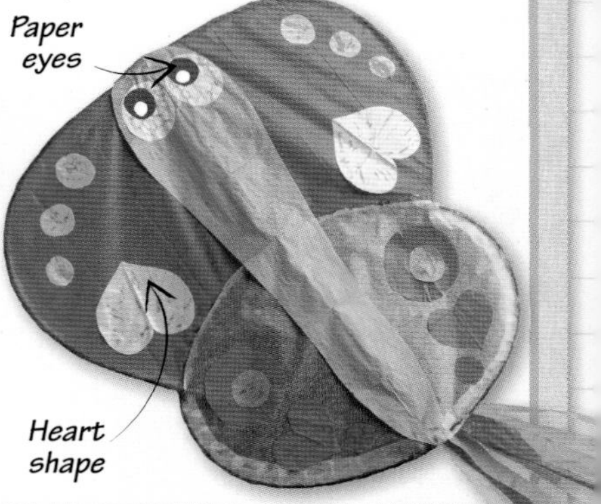

038 Test your kite-flying skills

30 MINS

Put your back to the wind, hold up the kite by the bridle line with one hand, let it catch the breeze, then let out the reel line. As the kite moves away, pull on the line to make it climb.

039 Reveal leaf skeletons

1 DAY

Deciduous leaves have veins that fan out from a large midrib attached to the stalk. The veins carry food to and from leaf cells. Remove the soft parts of the leaf to reveal its "skeleton" framework.

What you need
- Fallen leaves
- Rubber gloves
- Saucepan
- 1 litre (34 fl oz) water
- 40 g (1½ oz) washing soda
- Kitchen paper

1 Ask an adult to help. Add the water and washing soda to the saucepan. Heat until the mixture starts to boil.

2 Remove the pan from the heat. Carefully drop the leaves into the solution. Leave them to soak for several hours.

3 Wearing the gloves, put the pan under cold running water, and rinse the leaves thoroughly. Washing reveals the veiny skeleton. Dry off with kitchen paper.

Take care not to splash hot washing soda on your skin.

040 Take leaf rubbings

10 MINS

Put a leaf onto a smooth surface and cover it with white paper. Hold the paper down, rub over the leaf with a crayon or soft coloured pencil. Label each rubbing.

041 Make new lavender plants

20 MINS

Don't buy new plants every year – instead, take cuttings from an old plant and get them to make new roots. Snip off some lavender shoots in late summer, and you'll have several new plants next spring.

What you need

- *Lavender plant*
- *Small pots* • *Cutting compost* • *Scissors*
- *Plastic bag* • *Water*
- *Watering can*

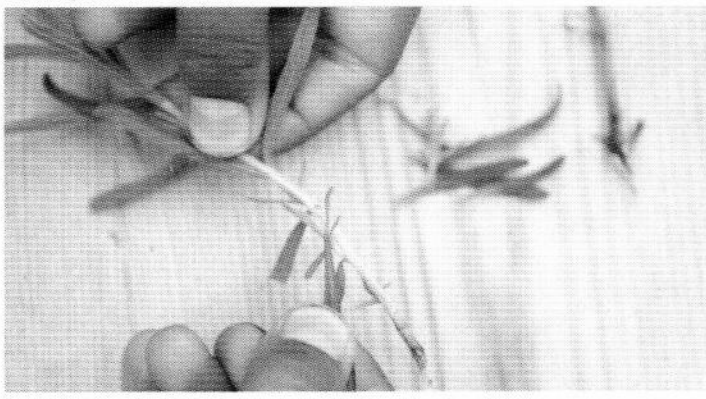

1 Find some new growth and cut the stem at an angle just below a leaf. Trim it to 10 cm (4 in). Fill a pot with compost.

2 Remove the lowest leaves until about four remain. Push the cutting into the pot, water it, and let it drain.

3 Cover the pot with a bag. Put it in a light place, out of direct sunlight. When new leaves form, move it into a new pot.

042 Make herb oil

30 MINS

Cut rosemary sprigs, wash them, and pat dry with kitchen paper. Lightly crush them. Put them in a dry, sterilized bottle (ask an adult to help). Fill it with olive oil, and use after a week.

043 Plant a hanging basket

1 HR

A hanging basket is really a garden in miniature. Make your own and you can choose the colours and types of plants you want to put in it. Keep it well watered and it should give you weeks of colourful blooms.

What you need
- Wire hanging basket • Sphagnum moss • Plastic bin liner • Plants • Compost

1 Line the basket with a thick layer of moss, then cut a piece of bin liner to fit the basket and line it with this. Trim the edges of the liner level with the moss.

2 Make some holes around the base and, working from the outside, insert some plants roots-first. Fill the base with compost.

3 Put more plants around the sides and on top, filling gaps with compost. Water the basket and hang it in a place where you can see and water it easily.

044 Make a hanging flower ball

45 MINS

Push a wire through a ball of floral foam. Twist a loop at the top and tie a ribbon to it. Wrap the other end around a small twig for support. Hang, and push the flowers into the foam.

045 Make a shell showcase

20 MINS

The next time you visit a beach and collect shells, why not show them off in this easy-to-make showcase? Be sure to rinse and dry your shells first, then identify them and make some labels to go in your showcase.

What you need
- *Thin card*
- *Pen or pencil*
- *Ruler*
- *Scissors*
- *Tape* • *Labels*

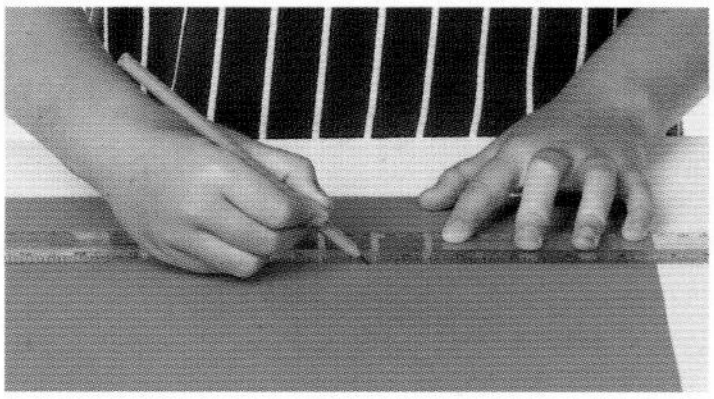

1 Draw and cut out a rectangle of card 40 x 30 cm (16 x 12 in). Mark off a margin of 2.5 cm (1 in) along all four sides.

2 Cut into the corners. Fold along the margin to make four sides. Tape the corners. Cut eight strips of card 2.5 cm (1 in) wide.

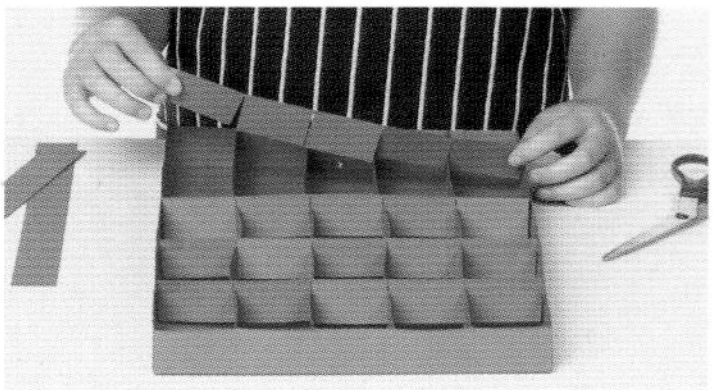

3 Fix four strips in the box with tape. Snip almost through the other strips to make compartments. Tape into place.

Identify and label your shells

046 Try beach long jump

5 MINS

Take advantage of a sandy beach to try out your skills in the long jump. Draw a line – this is your jump line and you're not allowed to go over it. Take a good run up to it and jump! Try again and see if you can go even farther.

047 Keep a nature journal

1 HR

Good naturalists keep a notebook or journal. Writing about what you see, hear, and smell when nature-watching helps you remember what you found. Include sketches, photos, leaves, feathers, and flowers.

What you need

• Blank notebook or notepad • Pencil, pen, watercolours, or paints of your choice • Tape • Binoculars

1 Go out and watch a plant, bird, or animal. Note down its appearance, behaviour, surroundings. Use all your senses. What can you hear? See? Smell?

Don't forget your hat!

2 Sketch your subject: note colours and distinctive marks. Tape any finds, such as leaves or feathers, to your journal pages.

3 Come back at other times of the year and note any changes.

Leaf specimen

048 Start a leaf collection

30 MINS

Keep a record of trees and bushes by collecting their leaves. Find as many types as you can, tape or glue them onto paper, then identify them.

Autumn leaves add colour

049 Make a water-balloon piñata

20 MINS

A piñata is usually a container filled with treats that fall out when it's hit by a blindfolded player and breaks open. Try this hot-weather version instead – the surprise "treat" is a soaking!

What you need

• Water balloons • Strong twine or rope • Funnel • Water • Foam bat or cardboard tube • Blindfold

1 Ask an adult to help you tie the twine or rope between two points so that it is about 0.6–1 m (2–3 ft) above the players.

2 Hold the neck of a balloon over the funnel and fill it slowly with water. Tie it off in a knot. The fuller the balloon, the easier it is to burst.

3 Tie each balloon to another length of twine. Add as many as you think the twine can take, then tie it to the middle of the piece you fixed in step 1.

4 Blindfold the first player, who will take one swing. Blindfold the next player and continue until all the balloons have burst.

050 Hit targets with water balloons

20 MINS

Set up some targets – these can be plastic bowls, buckets, hoops, or drinks bottles. Fill some water balloons, tie them off, and see who can hit the most targets.

Try not to get splashed!

051 Create a flower flick book

30 MINS

Make a flick book of a seed sprouting and you can watch it "growing" whenever you like! Draw a different growth stage in the same place on each page – these act like movie frames when you flick the pages.

What you need
- 3 sheets of A4 paper
- Stapler
- Scissors
- Coloured pens or pencils

1 Fold each piece of paper in half, then in half again to make four equal squares. Cut them out and staple together.

2 Make your first drawing. A flowerpot will be easy to trace onto the other sheets.

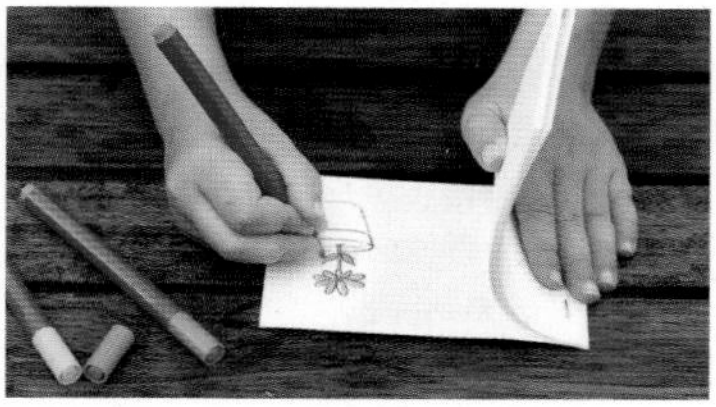

3 Draw a different growth stage on each page. Show the seedling break the ground, sprout leaves, then flower. Flick to watch your plant "grow".

Flick the pages to see your "movie"

052 Trim a grass hairstyle

10 MINS

Plant some decorative grass in a flowerpot. Glue on a face, then try out some different "hairstyles" on your plant person as the grassy hair grows.

Cut it long or short

053 Take a footprint plaster cast

1 HR

Many wild animals only come out at night, to avoid predators. Often they leave signs of their presence in the form of tracks – and you can preserve these to keep a record of their visits.

What you need
- *Thin card strip 25 x 4 cm (10 x 1½ in)* • *Water*
- *Paperclips* • *Mixing bowl*
- *Plaster of Paris*
- *Spoon* • *Toothbrush*

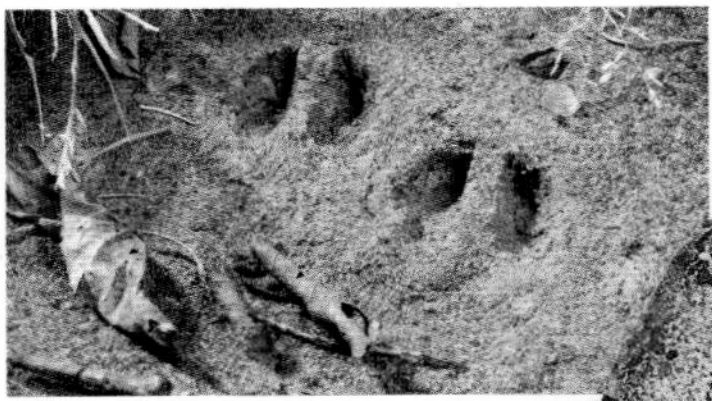

1 Find tracks in soft mud or wet woodland soil. Choose clear ones with the best outlines.

2 Make a ring with the card and fix it with a paperclip. Push the ring into the soil around the track. Mix the plaster to a smooth paste and pour it into the ring.

Match up the print

3 Leave to set for 30 minutes until it's hard enough to lift. Take it home and let it dry for 24 hours. Brush off any dirt, then use a guide to identify the animal.

054 Identify animal droppings

5 MINS

Black, tube-shaped droppings, or "scat", might belong to a fox. Thin, black tubes could be from a cat. Pellet-types are probably from deer or rabbits.

055 Build a birdwatching hide

40 MINS

Wild creatures, including birds, are naturally shy of humans. Making a hide will allow you to watch the animals in your garden without them even knowing you're there.

What you need
• 8 canes • String • Scissors • Dark-green mesh or netting • Leafy branches • Binoculars • Clothes pegs

1 Make the hide frame: tie the canes together with string to form a tent-like structure. Tie them tightly to prevent wobbling.

2 Drape the mesh over the frame. Attach it to the frame with pegs so that it doesn't flap in the wind.

3 Poke branches through the mesh to camouflage the hide. Cut some peepholes at eye level. Take your binoculars inside and see who shows up!

Birds only see binoculars

Make notes and sketches – they'll help you learn more about animals.

056 Camouflage yourself

5 MINS

Gather some leafy branches, lie on the ground, and cover up. Stay still and you'll be able to watch birds without them noticing.

Brace yourself on your elbows

057 Make a grapefruit geode

2 HRS

Geodes are dull-looking rocks, but crack one open and you'll find sparkling crystals inside. Make one by using a grapefruit as the "rock" and a chemical called alum for the crystals.

What you need
- Grapefruit • Spatula
- Foil • Plaster of Paris
- Goggles • Gloves • Alum
- Hot water • Food dye
- Measuring jug and scales

1 Remove the flesh from half a grapefruit, and line with foil. Mix a cupful of plaster in a bowl following the instructions.

2 Leave it until thick, then spread it over the foil with a spatula to make a thick layer. Put on the goggles and gloves.

3 Sprinkle in some alum and leave to harden. In a jug, add 100 g (3½ oz) of alum and food dye to 300 ml (10 fl oz) of hot water. Stir well and leave to cool.

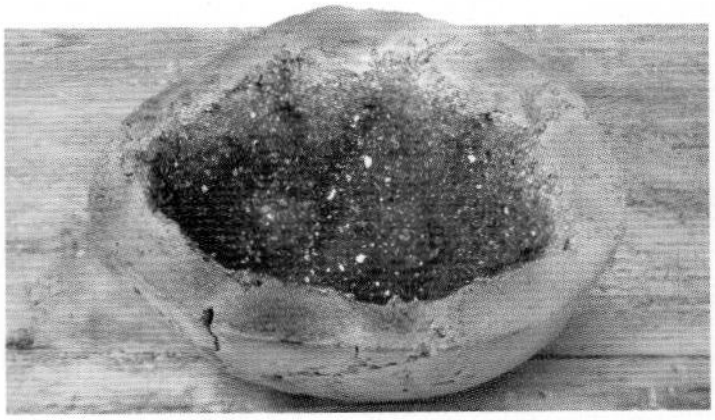

4 Fill the grapefruit with the solution. Over the next week, add any leftover solution. Leave your geode to dry into crystals, then peel off the grapefruit skin.

058 Make some slime

15 MINS

Tip a cup of cornflour into a bowl. Add some green food colouring to a ½ cup of water, then slowly stir into the cornflour. Add more cornflour and roll the mixture into a ball, like dough. When you stop, it "melts" between your fingers.

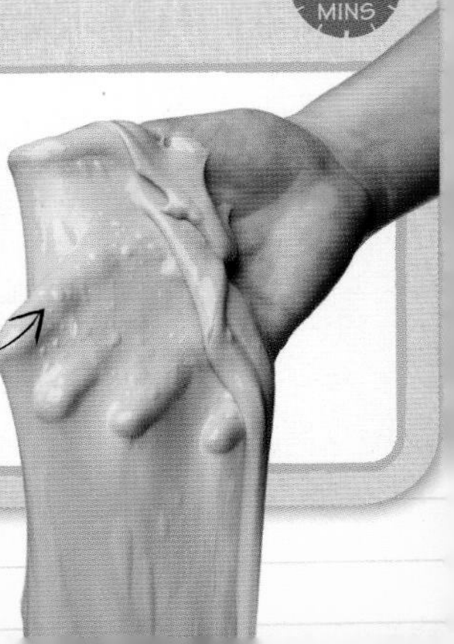

Slime becomes sticky and stretchy

059 Make a pine-cone wreath

45 MINS

The next time you're outdoors, pick up some pine cones. They're great for making decorations, such as this wreath. Add flowers, nuts, baubles, and glitter to give it a festive look.

What you need
- *Grapevine, raffia, or willow wreath*
- *Florist's wire* • *Wire cutters* • *Selection of pine cones*

1 Sort out some cones that are roughly the same size. Get an adult to cut the wire for you. Wrap a piece of wire around the base of each cone and give it a twist. Leave two tails for fixing to the wreath.

2 Start by putting cones all around the edge of your wreath. Tie them in with the wire. Once the circle is complete, fill in with more cones.

3 Add dried flowers, nuts, or some colourful ribbon if you like. Attach a loop of wire to the back for hanging.

060 Create a pine-cone animal

20 MINS

Turn a pine cone into a mouse. Cut some ears out of felt and glue them to a long acorn. Draw or paint on some eyes, a nose, and a mouth. Glue the acorn head to the top of a cone. Add a piece of string for a tail.

061 Make some bird food

30 MINS

Putting food out for birds is a great way to tempt them into your garden. Good-quality food also keeps them healthy in winter when wild food is scarce.

What you need
• 60 g (2 oz) lard • 125 g (4 oz) mix of unsalted nuts, oats, birdseed, grated cheese, brown breadcrumbs • Small stick • Yogurt pot • Scissors • Mixing bowl • Wooden spoon • Saucepan

1 Mix the scraps and seeds in a bowl. Ask an adult to melt the lard in a saucepan over a low heat. Pour it over the scraps. Stir well.

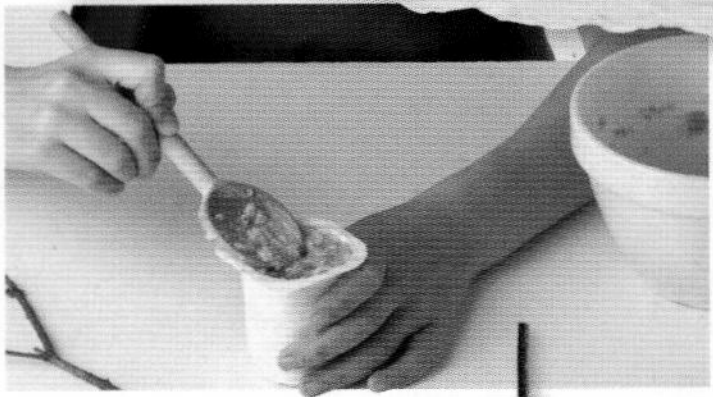

2 Spoon the mixture into the pot. Push in the stick, and leave to set.

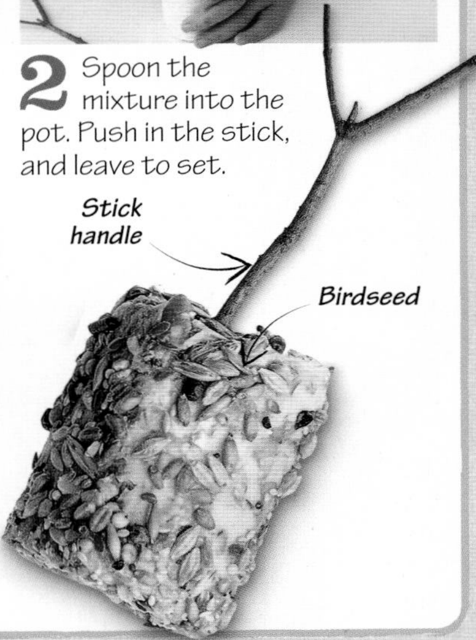

3 Once the mixture sets hard, pull it out of the pot by the stick. Roll it in more birdseed. Tie a piece of string to the stick, then hang it up outside.

062 Make different types of bird food

10 MINS

Push the lard mix into a fir cone and hang it once set. String nuts and nut shells with a needle. Hang a coconut half from string. When the coconut is eaten, fill it with lard mix.

063 Bob for some apples

20 MINS

Apple bobbing is a game traditionally played at Halloween or harvest time, but you can play it any time you have enough apples – and some friends who don't mind getting wet!

What you need

• Apples • A big bowl or tub – anything large enough to fit your head in • Sturdy table • Water • Towels

1 Put the bowl or tub on a sturdy table that's about waist-high. Fill it with cool (not cold) water about three-quarters full.

2 Float several apples in the water. You want them to move – this makes the game more challenging.

3 Put your hands behind your back. Have someone say "Go!" Try to grab an apple with your mouth in 20–30 seconds, then it's the next player's turn.

064 Juggle apples

1 HR

Hold an apple in each hand. Throw apple one up and across to hand two. Before you catch it, throw apple two under and across to hand one. Catch apple two, and repeat until perfect.

Once you master two, move on to three!

065 Bury a beetle bucket

45 MINS

Many beetles need a moist forest floor full of decaying wood and leaves to live in. Sadly, some are vanishing due to habitat loss. This beetle bucket could help your local beetles to survive.

What you need
- Plastic bucket
- Craft knife • Stones
- Bark chippings
- Spade • Logs
- Garden soil

1 Cut 3 cm (1 in) holes in the sides and base of the bucket for entryways. Choose a patch of ground that won't be disturbed.

2 Bury the bucket in a deep hole. Put large stones in the bottom, then add one or two logs (oak is best), standing on end.

3 Fill the bucket with bark chippings, then a little soil. Female beetles will lay their eggs on the logs, and the larvae will eat the wood as it decays.

4 Put some logs on top of the bucket to mark the site and leave the area undisturbed. Other beetles will use the logs on top, as well as those in the bucket.

066 Tell a bug from a beetle

5 MINS

There are over 350,000 different types of beetles. Most have hard wing cases that hide their hind wings. Their mandibles are used for chewing food rather than sucking up liquid like a bug.

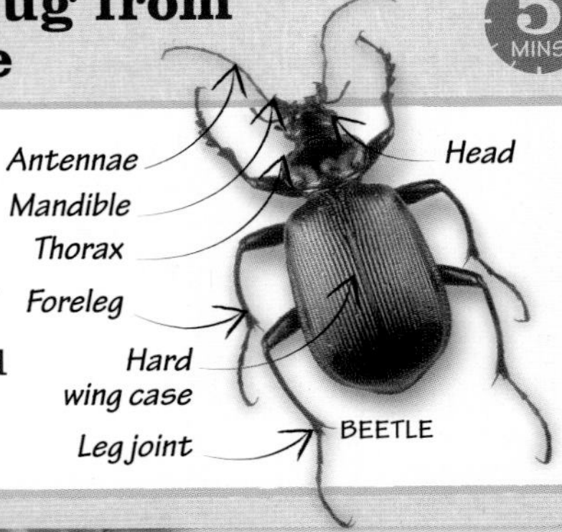

067 Start a rock collection

1 HR

What you need
- A keen eye
- Field guide to rocks and minerals
- Magnifying glass

A rock collection is easy to start – rocks are all around you. First check out the rocks in your drive, garden, or on beaches or riverbanks. Try to identify your favourites, then compare them with ones you find further away.

1 Divide your collected rocks into groups. Think about colour, size, or where you collected them.

2 Use a magnifying glass to inspect your rock. Is it smooth or grainy? Does it contain crystals? Also look for layers, veins, bubbles, or cracks.

3 Make a display case or specimen tray for your best finds. As you identify them, add a label in each compartment so that you know what rock it is. You might choose to have a tray for crystals and another for green minerals, for instance.

Add labels to each of your specimens

068 Make a specimen tray

15 MINS

Cut thin cardboard into a square. Cut small squares out of each corner to make side flaps. Fold up each flap and tape together. Cut out small boxes to tape inside as compartments.

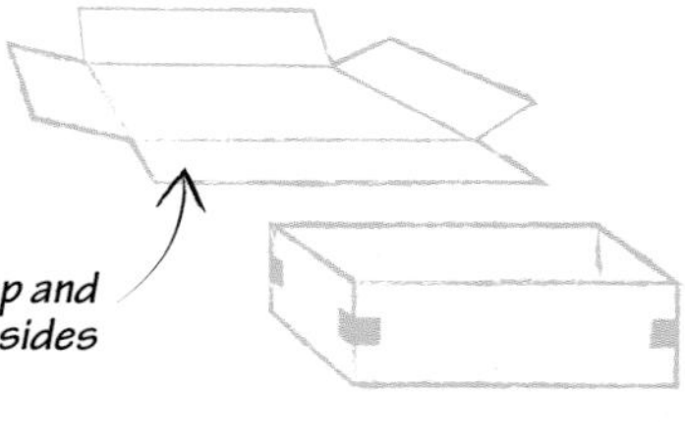

Fold up and tape sides

069 Make herb and flower ice cubes

20 MINS

Freezing plants is one of the easiest ways to preserve them for future use. You can give lemonade an extra-special touch with flower-filled ice cubes, or chop up summer herbs for use in the winter.

What you need

- Edible flowers (violas or borage) or herbs (mint, parsley, lemon verbena)
- Water
- Ice-cube tray

1 Choose the flowers and herbs you want to freeze. Chop green herbs, or use just one leaf per cube. Use one small whole flower in each ice cube.

2 Put your herbs or flowers into each cube and fill with water. Try star shaped or other ice-cube shapes to make even more of an impact.

3 Put the tray into the freezer. When frozen, use the flower and leaf cubes in summer drinks. Keep the chopped herbs for soups and stews.

070 Make it frosty

10 MINS

Put crushed ice into a glass. Add salt to melt it. As the ice melts, it cools the glass, and water in the air forms frost crystals that cling to the outside.

071 Take mushroom spore prints

15 MINS

Fungi produce white, yellow, or black spores. Single spores are hard to see, but you can take a print of a whole mushroom. Use lighter or darker card if the print is difficult to see clearly.

What you need
- Mature mushroom (from supermarket)
- Coloured card
- Glass bowl
- Artist's fixative spray

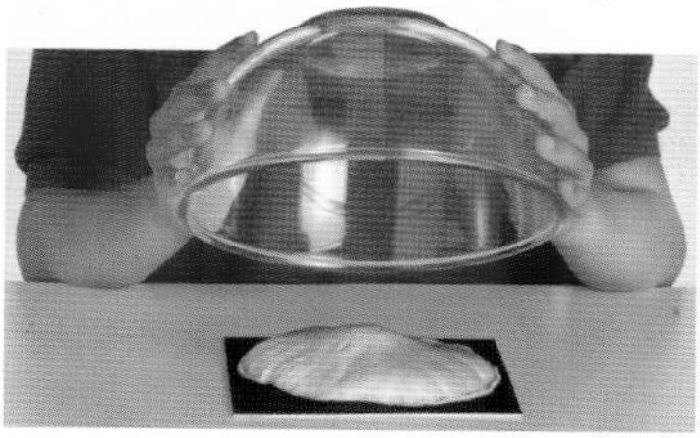

1 Place a mushroom cap, gill- or pore-side down, on a piece of card. Put the bowl over it to protect it from draughts.

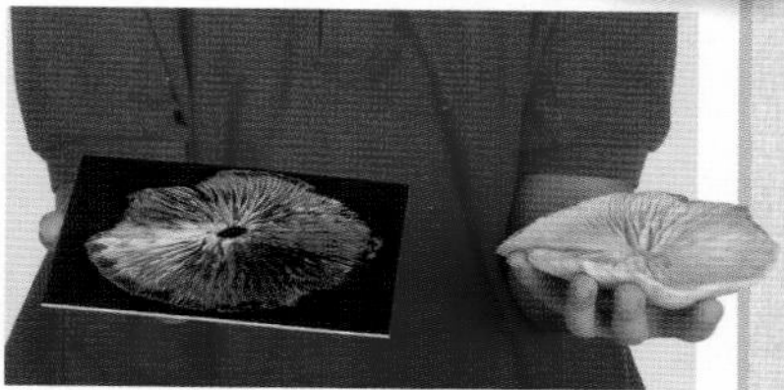

2 Leave overnight, then carefully lift the cap from the card. You should now have a spore print.

3 Be careful not to touch it or it will smudge. Spray the print with fixative in a well-ventilated room or outdoors, to stop the spores from rubbing off.

White spore print

072 Make stamps with mushrooms

15 MINS

Cut a mushroom cap in half. Dip it into paint or ink and press it gently onto a sheet of paper. By linking the stamps, you can create patterns and different designs.

Use two colours

073 Decorate your garden with butterflies

40 MINS

What you need
- Clean foil containers
- Scissors
- Black and coloured markers
- Ballpoint pen
- Glue
- Wooden skewers

Gardening isn't all about plants. It's a chance to have fun and be creative, too. Make these colourful foil butterflies and add some sparkle to your borders.

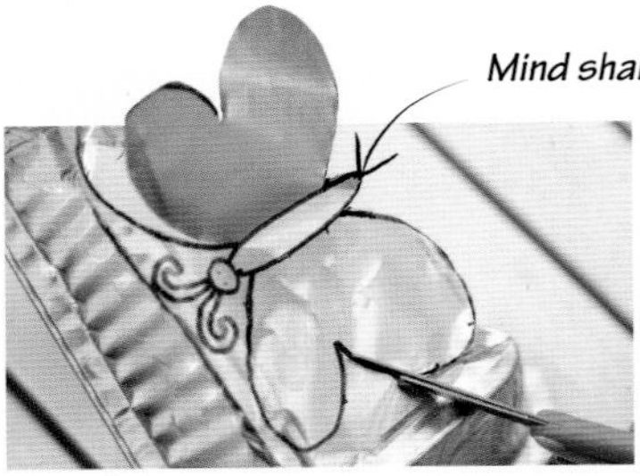

1 Use a black marker to draw your butterfly design on the base of a container. Cut out the design with a pair of scissors.

2 Press a ballpoint pen head into the design to make a raised pattern. Add colour using the coloured markers. Let it dry.

3 Put glue on a stick and press down until it's secure. Let it dry. Find the best place in your garden to show off your artwork!

074 Make some pebble pets

25 MINS

Gather some pebbles and wash them. Glue small pebbles to larger ones to make frogs and pigs. Use felt ears and a string tail to make a mouse. Paint them and add googly eyes.

075 Go on a nature hunt

40 MINS

You don't need to live in a forest to have a nature hunt. With a little observation you can find loads of animals and plants in your back garden. Get your friends together and see who can find the most.

What you need
- Hunt checklists – as many as there are hunters
- Pencils or pens

1 First, make a checklist of what you think you might find. Put a box next to each one so you can tick them off. Start with small creatures – ants and woodlice – or common plants, such as clover.

2 Don't forget that nature is all around you, all the time. You might hunt for specific birds, animals, or insects, or you may want to focus on different types of trees or even clouds.

3 Hunt bugs under rocks or logs. Look for birds on the ground or in trees. Use all your senses – is there a flower scent on your list? Set a time limit, and see who has the most boxes ticked.

Fill in your checklist as you go

076 Lie down and listen

15 MINS

Lie down outdoors on a grassy hill or under a tree. Close your eyes and keep as still as you can. What do you hear? Trees creaking in the wind? Squirrels chattering? Birdsong? Just listen...

What sounds can you hear?

077 Make leaf flowers

15 MINS

When can one plant turn into another? When you transform garden leaves into these beautiful long-stemmed "roses". It's a pretty way to recycle fallen leaves if they're not too dry.

What you need

- *Sycamore or maple leaves*
- *A stick*
- *Thin garden wire*
- *Wire cutters*

1 Hold a smaller leaf by the stem, vein-side up. Fold the top down to meet the stalk, then fold in the sides to make a "bud".

2 Take another leaf, fold it over, then wrap it around the bud. Hold the leaf stems against the stick as you repeat this.

3 Keep adding leaves until your flower is the size you want, then wrap wire around the leaf stems to fix them to the stick. Make several for a "bouquet".

078 Stencil a ripening fruit

1 MIN

If you have fruit trees in your garden, find a fruit such as an apple, that is full-size but not yet ripe. Put a sticker shape on it. As the fruit ripens, the area under the sticker will stay pale.

079 Make a weather front

15 MINS

When a warm and a cool mass of air meet, they create a boundary, or "front" between them. You can't see this happening in air, but you can make a front in a jar to see how it works.

What you need
- Large glass jar
- Jug
- Hot (not boiling) water
- Cold water
- Green food dye
- Thermometer

1 Fill the jar with cold water until just over half-full. Fill the jug with hot water. Add a few drops of food dye and stir.

2 Tip the jar of cold water so that the water is close to the rim. Now slowly pour the green hot water down the jar's neck.

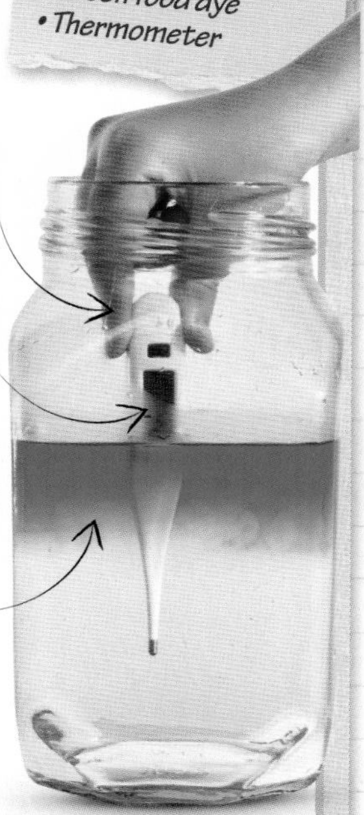

Hold the thermometer carefully

Test the temperatures of the layers

"Weather front"

3 The warm green water forms a layer above the cold, heavier water. The area where they meet is like a weather front.

080 Make a rainbow

2 MINS

Make a rainbow in your back garden. Stand with the Sun behind you. Set the hose on fine spray and slowly move it around until you see a rainbow appear.

Water droplets reflect and split sunlight into colours

081 Build your own barometer

45 MINS

As air gets hotter or colder, it causes changes in air pressure, altering weather patterns. Build a barometer to measure how the pressure changes in the air – and you can also predict the weather.

What you need
- Bowl • Large balloon
- Scissors • Tape
- 2 drinking straws
- Coloured cardboard
- Marker pens • Ruler

1 Cut off most of the round part of the balloon and stretch it tight over the bowl. Fix it securely with tape.

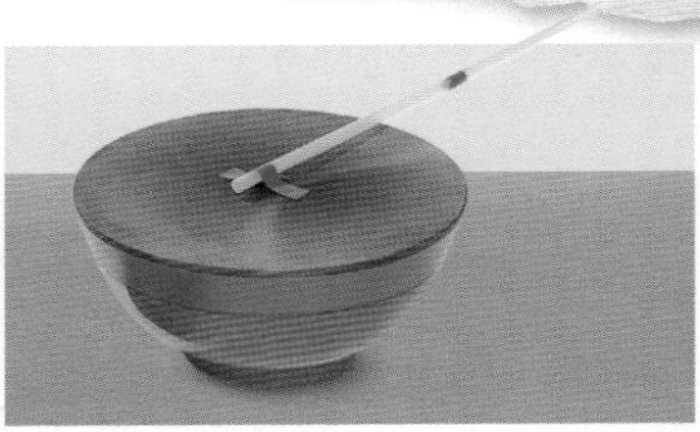

2 Slit the end of a straw, push it inside the other straw and tape together. Tape one end to the middle of the balloon.

3 Using your pen and ruler, mark a series of lines 6 mm (1/4 in) apart on a folded piece of card. Stand the scale by the end of the pointer.

4 Check it every few hours to see whether the pointer has moved up or down with changes in the air pressure. Up shows fine weather: down shows wet.

082 Measure hailstones

10 MINS

Centre a square block of 2.5 cm (1 in) thick foam on a large sheet of heavy foil, dull side up. Fold the foil over the edges and tape in place. Put the pad out when it hails and measure the dents.

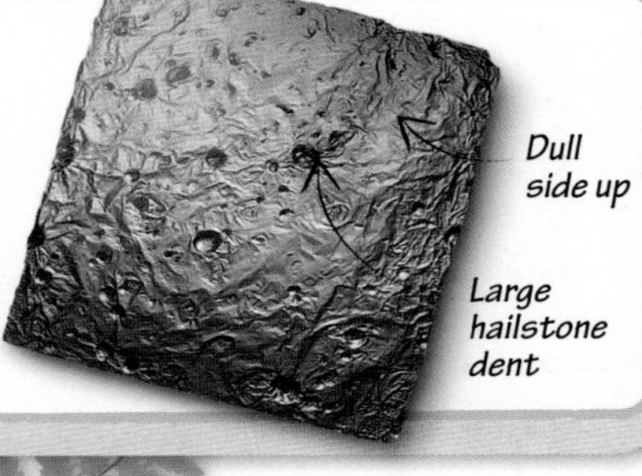

083 Make your own fertilizer

15 MINS

Weeds can help your garden grow if you turn them into fertilizer to feed the plants you really want. Even pesky weeds contain nutrients that are good for another plant's health. Don't throw them away!

What you need
- Bucket
- Rubber gloves
- 2 bricks
- Compost weeds
- Water
- Stick or cane as a stirrer

Large bucket

1 Put on your rubber gloves and gather a bunch of compost weeds, such as nettles, comfrey, docks, and horsetails. Shake off any soil and put them, roots and all, into a large bucket.

2 Weigh down the plants with bricks. Fill the bucket with water and stir it weekly. This part can get smelly!

3 After 3–5 weeks you'll have a gooey mass. Dilute it with water (1 part goo to 10 parts water) and use it weekly to water your plants. See how they grow!

084 Make leaf mould

20 MINS

Put fallen leaves in a bin bag. When it's almost full, spray the leaves with water. Tie the bag, punch in some holes, and store it in a shady spot. After a year, spread the rich leaf mould around your garden.

085 Make a grapefruit bug catcher

15 MINS

What you need
- Grapefruit • Spoon
- Notebook or digital camera • Pencil
- Paintbrush • Small plastic container

Leaf litter and soil are home to slugs, insects, spiders, worms, and other different types of invertebrate. Use this grapefruit trap to see how many you can find.

1 Ask an adult to cut the grapefruit in half. Use the spoon to scoop out the flesh (you can eat this later).

2 Put the grapefruit halves, upside down, on the ground in different sheltered places and leave them out overnight.

3 Turn over the skins. Use the paintbrush to gently push the animals into the container so you can identify them. Then let them go.

086 Be a bug detective

5 MINS

Use a magnifying glass to study insects up close. How many body parts do they have? How many legs? Can you see any pincers or spines?

087 Make a bubble wand

20 MINS

You may have seen professional bubble-wand performers in a park or street fair creating huge bubbles. Now you can do the same by making this giant bubble wand and bubble mixture.

What you need
- Wire hanger
- Washing-up liquid
- Glycerine • Water
- Large bowl
- Cling film • Tray

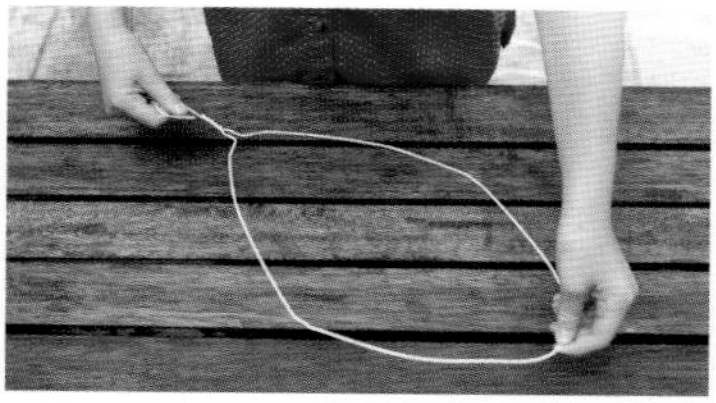

1 Pull the hanger into a circle. In a bowl, mix two parts glycerine to 15 parts washing-up liquid. Add 15 parts of water slowly. Stir gently.

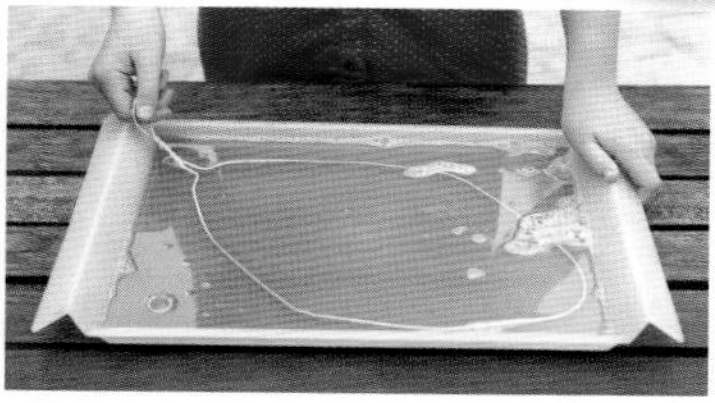

2 Cover the bowl and let the mixture rest for 2–3 days – the longer, the better. Pour it into a waterproof tray.

3 Dip your wand into the mixture, then swish it slowly and smoothly through the air. Make a number of wands to create different-sized bubbles.

088 Blow bubbles with your fingers

1 MIN

If the bubble mixture is thick enough, you can use your own fingers as a wand. Just put your thumb and index finger together in a circle shape, dip it in bubble mixture, and blow.

See how large you can make your bubbles!

089 Plant a Wild West garden

30 MINS

Saddle up and give a shallow container a touch of the Old West with prickly cacti and other desert plants. Because their stems store water, cacti can survive if you miss a watering.

What you need
- Container • Gravel
- Cactus compost
- Spoon • Trowel
- Tongs • Gloves
- Cacti • Sand • Water

1 Fill the base of the container with a thin layer of gravel. Add 2–5 cm (1–2 in) of compost. Dig a few holes for your cacti.

2 Wearing the gloves, take a cactus from its pot. Use tongs to put it in its hole. Firm the soil around it with a spoon.

3 Plant the other cacti the same way. Lightly water the soil with lukewarm water. Add some models to make a scene.

090 Make a miniature garden

10 MINS

Fill a jar lid with kitchen paper or cotton wool. Dampen it with water. Drop on some cress seeds and tiny bits of gravel. Put in a model animal. Your "cress forest" will grow around it.

091 Help a bird build a nest

15 MINS

All birds need places to raise their young. Building a nest takes a lot of time and energy, but you can help them by putting out some of the things they need to make a home.

What you need

- *6 shallow dishes • Mud • Moss*
- *Twigs or pine needles • Straw, grass, dead leaves • Fur, hair, wool*
- *Short pieces of string or yarn*

1 Fill each bowl with one type of material. Put them in a visible but sheltered place where birds can see them.

2 Keep watch on the bowls from a distance. Do some birds prefer one material more than another?

092 Listen to the dawn chorus

15 MINS

Birds sing all year long, but dawn in spring is when they make the most noise, as males try to find mates and warn off rivals. Get up early to hear them, though – they can start singing at 4 a.m.!

093 Make an anemometer

30 MINS

Wind speed is measured with an anemometer, which rotates as the wind blows. Make this simple anemometer, count the number of turns, and you can work out wind speed for yourself.

What you need
- 4 small paper cups
- Small paper plate • Pen
- Ruler • Pencil with eraser
- Drawing pin • Double-sided tape • Coloured tape

1 Use the ruler and pen to mark an X on the paper plate. Put a band of coloured tape around one of the cups.

2 Tape each cup to the plate, facing the same way, so that the centre sits at the end of a line.

3 Pin the centre of the plate to the pencil eraser so that it turns easily. Hold it up in the wind. Count the number of turns the banded cup makes in a minute.

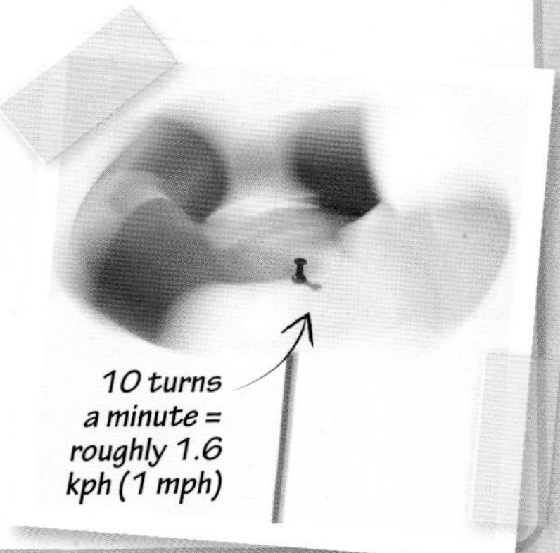

10 turns a minute = roughly 1.6 kph (1 mph)

094 Have a raindrop race

3 MINS

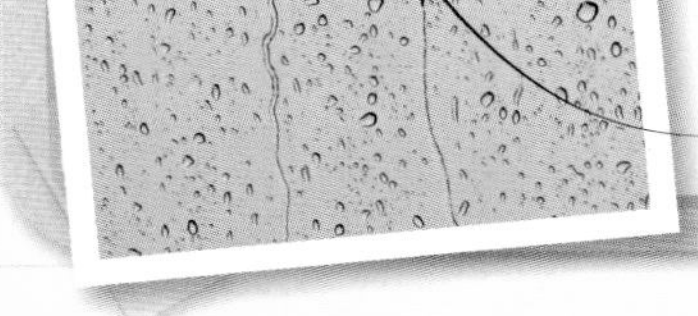

The next time it rains, have a raindrop race with a friend. Each of you chooses a large raindrop at the top of a window. The one that reaches the bottom first is the winner!

See which raindrop wins

095 Make a feather crown

30 MINS

From Native Americans to Polynesian islanders, cultures all over the world use feathers to make headdresses. You can, too, with a bit of willow and feathers you've found in the countryside.

What you need

- *Feathers*
- *Long pieces of bendy willow or wisteria vine*

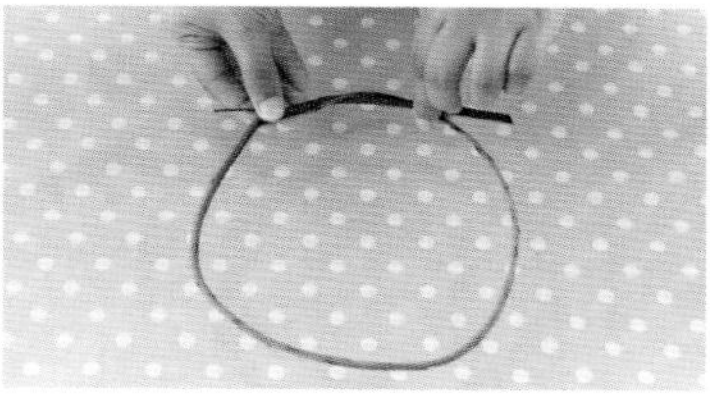

1 Make a circle of willow that fits your head. Weave the ends underneath each other to hold it in place.

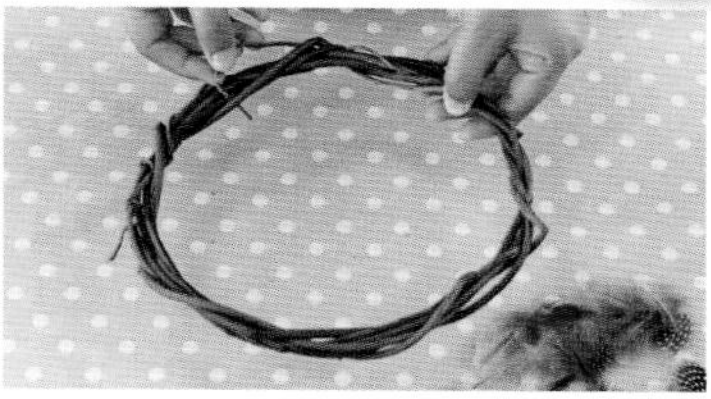

2 Wrap more stems or vines in and around the circle. Push the ends beneath the stems to fix in place.

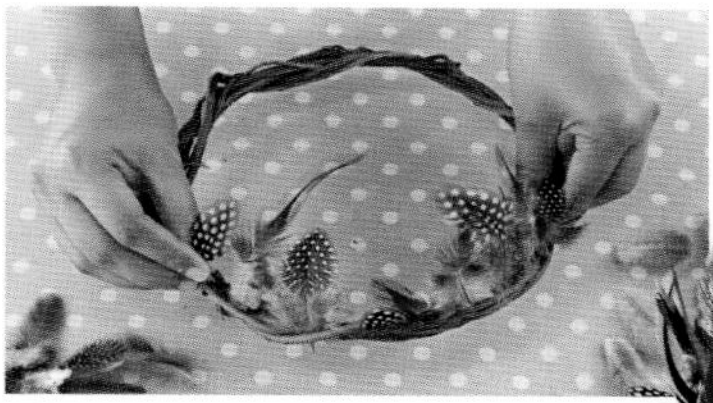

3 Gently push the feather quills in between the stems. Try putting a larger one at the front and smaller ones around the sides.

096 Write with a quill pen

15 MINS

Ask an adult to cut a feather into a flat point with a small slit up the middle. Hold the quill at 45°, dip it into ink or food colouring and tap off any excess. Write as lightly as you can. Dip and repeat.

097 Build a log-pile home

30 MINS

What you need
- *Spade*
- *Logs and sticks*
- *Bark, leaves, and some ivy plants*

Rotting wood is important for wildlife, and there's lots going on in a log pile. It provides food for some animals and insects, while others use it as a place to hibernate during winter. Once built, don't disturb it.

1 Pick a shady corner that's out of the way – dappled shade is best. Dig a shallow pit. Pile up the logs, the biggest at the bottom.

2 Put the smaller sticks on top, crisscrossing them as you go. Fill any spaces with leaves, bark, pine cones, or stones.

3 Plant an ivy vine and trail it across the top of the pile to help keep in moisture. Your log pile will now make a warm, safe home for small creatures.

Lichens, mosses, and fungi also grow on log piles and provide food for bugs.

098 Make a maze for woodlice

20 MINS

Use building bricks to make a maze that has a T-junction. Put in some woodlice and let them wander around. Add a brick to make them turn right, then let them choose. Most will turn left!

099 Make a mistletoe ball

1 HR

Ivy and mistletoe are traditional Christmas decorations that will look fantastic in this "kissing ball". Grab some ivy from the garden, and finish with mistletoe from a garden centre.

!

What you need
- Florist's wire
- Ivy • Mistletoe
- Apple • Ribbon
- Red mini baubles
- Duct tape

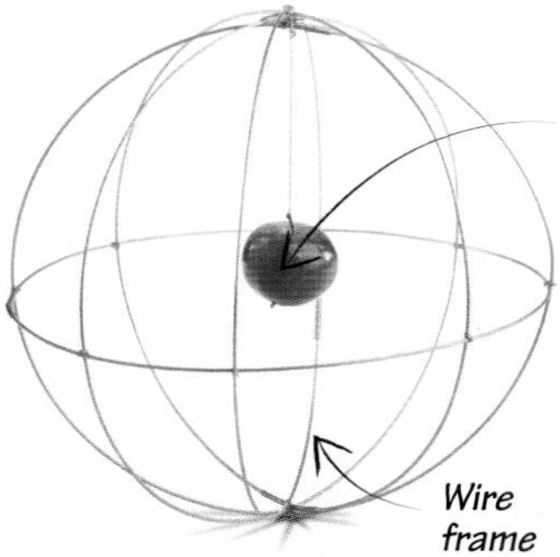

1 Ask an adult to help you make a sphere out of the florist's wire. Either twist or tape the wires together.

2 Suspend the apple in the centre of the sphere on a separate wire. Push it through the apple and twist to hold. Weave ivy all through the sphere. Add mini baubles if you like. Attach a bunch of mistletoe to the base, add ribbons, and hang up.

100 Make a festive bough

30 MINS

Find a bare branch from the garden and ask an adult to help you spray paint it silver. Suspend it from wire over a doorway. Hang lightweight decorations on it for some extra Christmas cheer.

Make it look festive

101 Spread some seed hitchhikers

45 MINS

Plants spread seeds in many ways. Many "hitchhike" on passing birds, insects, and animals – including humans. After your next nature walk, why not see what seeds may have come home with you?

What you need
- Metal baking tray
- Oven gloves
- Seed compost
- Blunt knife or screwdriver
- Cling film
- Watering can

1 Preheat the oven to 100°C (210°F). Fill the baking tray with compost and bake it for 30 minutes to kill any hidden seeds.

2 Remove the tray from the oven with oven gloves. Let it cool. Use the knife to scrape your shoe soles over the compost.

3 Water it with a fine spray, put cling film over the top, then set it on a sunny windowsill. Any hitchhiking seeds should sprout within 10 days.

102 Plant a sock

10 MINS

Put some old socks over your shoes and take a walk around the garden. Remove the socks, put them in a foil tray, add some compost, and water lightly. See what plants spring up!

103 Play a flying disc game

1 HR

Try throwing and catching a flying disc, then play a game of "Ultimate". Pass the disc to your teammates to catch it inside the other team's end zone – but no running when you have the disc!

What you need
- A flying disc
- Friends
- Open place to play, free of trees, like an open park, beach, or sports field
- Practice!

1 To master the backhand throw, grip the disc so that your index finger is on the rim, your thumb is on top, and the rest of your fingertips are just touching the underside.

2 Standing sideways, face your friend. Curl your wrist towards your body, with your elbow pointing up and out. Keep the disc level with your waist to make it fly straight.

3 Quickly fling your arm out, flicking or "snapping" your wrist and releasing the disc when your arm is almost fully extended.

4 To play Ultimate, divide into two teams. Mark two end zones. You score when you catch the disc in the other team's zone.

104 Try paper keepy-uppies

20 MINS

Scrunch up some scrap paper into a ball. See how long you can keep it in the air without using your hands. Bounce it with your knees and ankles like a professional footballer, or use your head – anything goes, except hands!

105 Create a pressed flower picture

30 MINS

What you need
- *Pressed flowers*
- *Tweezers* • *Paper*
- *Scissors* • *Clear self-adhesive cover film* • *Cocktail stick*
- *Glue* • *Bottle tops*

Pressed flowers are pretty to look at by themselves, but put several together and you can make a picture out of them. Try making this bouquet and hang it on your wall to enjoy all year round.

1 Cut a piece of white paper the size you want your picture. Start to arrange the flowers using tweezers.

2 Pour glue in a bottle top. Use a cocktail stick to put a tiny drop where you want to fix a flower. When ready, cut the film to the same size as the paper.

3 Peel off the backing and carefully place the film over the picture. Press down gently. Your picture is ready to frame.

106 Hang flowers to dry

15 MINS

Remove any damaged leaves from the flowers. Tie them into small bunches with string and hang them upside down in a warm, dry place for 1–2 weeks. They're ready when dry to the touch.

107 Make a leaf wreath

20 MINS

You can make a wreath at any time of year by using leaves. Choose green ones for spring, or gather fallen ones for autumn – they'll be more brittle, so be gentle!

What you need
- *Garden wire cut to the size you want your wreath to be (ask an adult to help)*
- *Leaves*

1 Twist a loop at one end of the wire to hold the leaves on. Carefully push the other end through the centre of a leaf.

2 String other leaves in the same way, pushing them down to meet the first. Try to keep them facing the same way.

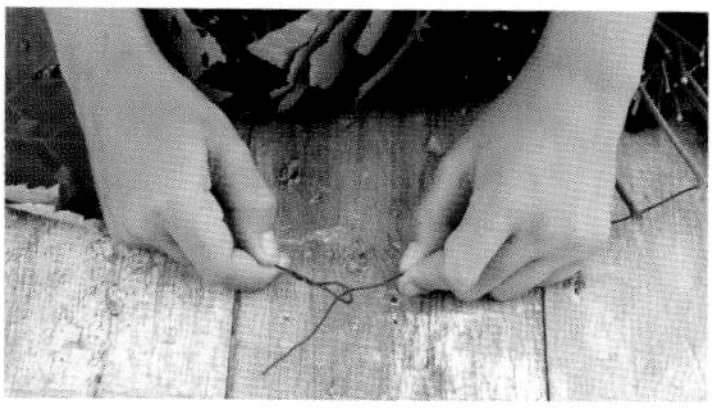

3 When you've used all the leaves, put the other end of the wire through the loop. Pull it gently into a circle, and use the excess wire to hang it up.

108 Hang leaf bunting

10 MINS

Choose some prettily shaped or coloured leaves from your garden. Tie a piece of twine between two branches, or use two drawing pins to tack it to a shed. Hang up the leaves with clothes pegs.

Festive leaves on a line

109 Compare leaf structure

20 MINS

All plants have leaves, but have you ever noticed how different they can be? A willow's are long and slender. An oak's are lobed. A pine's are needle-shaped, while a holly's have spiny edges. Find out the types in your garden.

What you need

- *The leaves in your garden or nearby park*

1 First, see if the leaf shape is simple or compound. A simple leaf has just one leaf to a stem, like an oak's. A compound leaf has several leaflets coming off a central stem, like the vine called Virginia creeper.

2 How are the leaves arranged? Some are solitary, but others form in clusters. Some grow opposite each other. Others alternate.

3 See what kind of textures your leaves have. Are they smooth and waxy, or coarse and rough? Do they have spiny bits or just crinkled edges?

110 Track some leaf colours

5 MINS

Leaves change colour as they grow and age. Most start out bright green but turn many different shades before they die. Photograph the same plant leaf every month for a year to see how it changes.

111 Make leaf lanterns

20 MINS

Transform some plain glass tealight holders – or even jam jars – into beautiful leaf lanterns. Simply stick on some pretty leaves, give them a coat of glue, and let the light shine through.

What you need
- Decorative leaves
- PVA craft glue and brush
- Tealights
- Clear tealight holders or jars

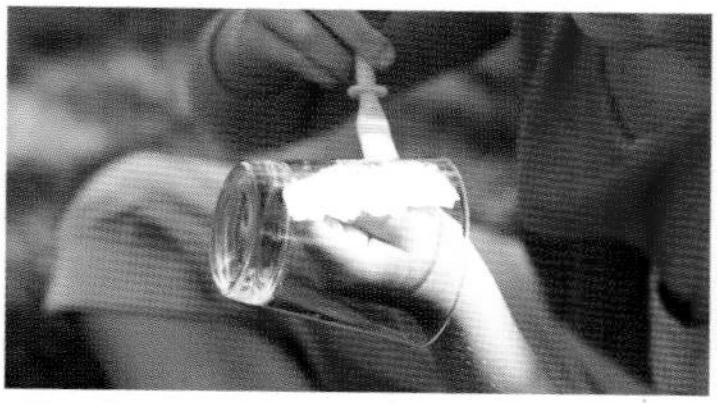

1 Flatten your leaves by pressing them underneath heavy books overnight. Coat the outside of the glass with glue.

2 Press on your leaves in any pattern you choose. If it's autumn, try to use red or gold ones, but any design will be pretty when it's lit by candlelight.

3 Paint another thick coat of PVA over the leaves. Let them dry thoroughly, then ask an adult to drop in a tealight and light it for you. They're great if you're having an evening party. Just remember – never leave a lit candle unattended, and blow it out when you're finished.

112 Make shadow creatures

5 MINS

Shine a torch or lamp on a wall. See how many shadows of different creatures you can make with your hands, using them one at a time or both together. Add sound effects if you like!

113 Make a chalk pavement picture

30 MINS

What you need

- *Coloured chalk*
- *Paving stones or patio*

You don't always need paper to draw pictures. Use your patio or garden path as a palette and you can create colourful chalk artworks that will wash away with the next rain shower.

Use different colours to make contrasts

1 Choose a smooth section of patio in a place where you won't have people stepping on your work. Ask permission first, though, and make sure that the chalk will wash off.

2 Decide what you want to draw. You could make one drawing in one place, or make a path out of flowers, stars, or fish, or trace around your hands to make a handprint picture.

3 Make your drawing as complicated or as easy as you like. The choice is yours! Then stand back and admire your artwork.

114 Trace someone's shadow

3 HRS

Trace a friend's shadow. Mark where your friend stood, then come back in an hour to see where the shadow falls. Repeat to see how the outline changes. Does your friend get taller or shorter?

This shadow is getting smaller

115 Play a garden memory game

20 MINS

Test your nature identification abilities with this great memory game. Match pairs of images and you'll improve your observational skills as you play. Why not make the cards out of your own photos?

What you need
- *Wildlife and plant images*
- *Card for backing*
- *Glue*

1 Find pictures of any plants and animals you see regularly in your garden. Print two copies of each and stick them on some card. You'll need at least 10–12 different species.

Pigeons can remember faces and will avoid people who shoo them away!

2 To play, shuffle the cards. Lay them face down. Each player takes turns to reveal two cards. If they match, the player keeps them. If not, the cards are turned over. Whoever has the most pairs wins.

3 Alternatively, take the cards outside and share them out. The first person to spot and name everything on their cards wins.

116 Dissect an owl pellet

40 MINS

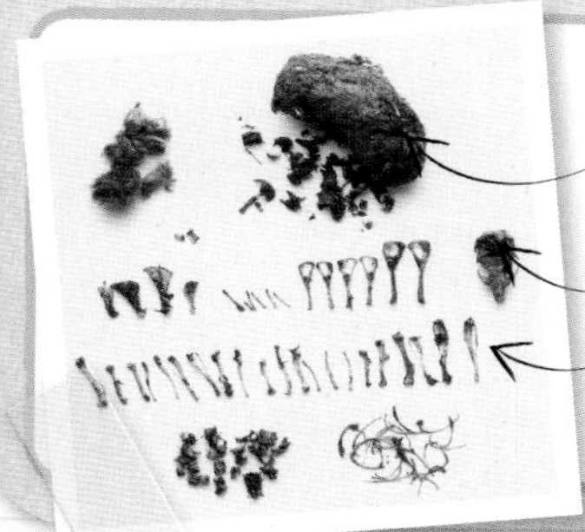

Break the pellet into two or three pieces, then soak them in water for an hour to soften. Use tweezers to tease them apart and find out what the owl has eaten.

117 Plant a fairy ring

1 HR

What you need
- 2 canes
- Long piece of string
- Spade
- Tape
- Compost
- Tall, scented flowers
- Ornamental grasses

Fairy rings aren't all about toadstools or mushrooms. Plant a secret fairy ring at the bottom of your garden using ornamental grasses and tall, sweet-smelling flowers, and you can create your own magical place.

1 Push a cane into the grass and tie one end of the string to it. Tie the other end to the second cane. Use it to mark out the ring.

2 Dig a trench around the ring and add some compost. Take each plant out of its pot, put it in the trench, and cover with soil.

3 Press down the soil and water the plants well. Hang lanterns, fairy lights, or other decorations around the ring.

118 Make a garden lantern

40 MINS

Paint a jam jar with some special glass paint, or use household paint and put a layer of varnish on top. When dry, wrap some wire around the top for hanging. Put a tealight inside and ask an adult to light it for you.

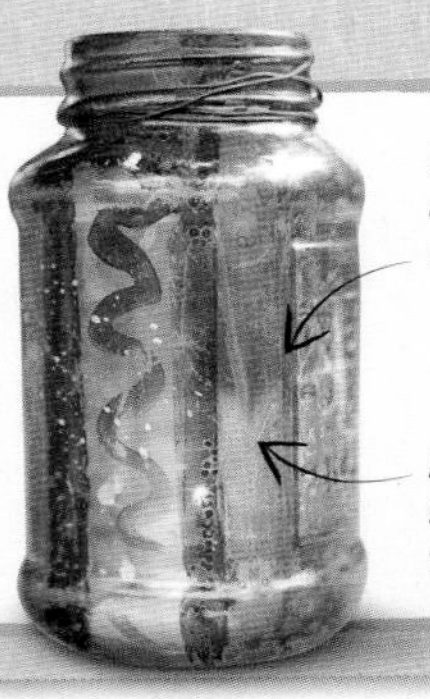

119 Make a wind vane

40 MINS

A wind vane faces the direction the wind is blowing from – not where it's going. Track shifting wind patterns by making this wind vane. Align coloured pegs to a compass and you'll know the exact direction.

What you need
- A4 sheet of stiff card
- Scissors
- Tape
- 2 pennies
- Pen top
- BBQ skewer
- Cane
- 4 clothes pegs

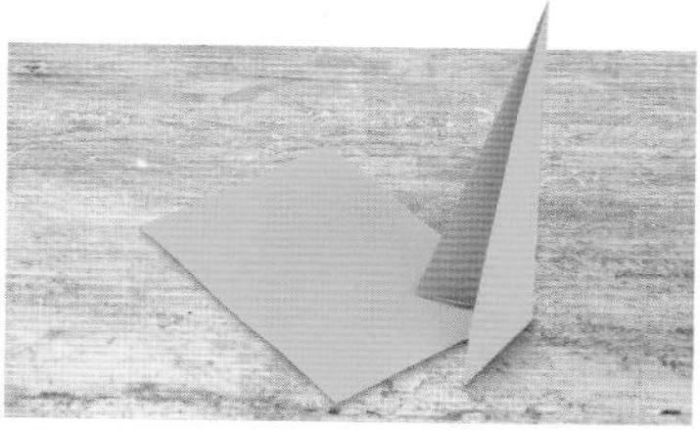

1 Fold the card in half lengthways. Draw from the bottom corner to the top centre fold and cut through both layers.

2 Tape the pennies inside near the tip. These will help to balance the vane when it's complete. Tape the vane shut.

3 Balance it on a pencil to find the balance point. Mark this point and tape the pen top to it. Tape the skewer to the cane and push it into the ground.

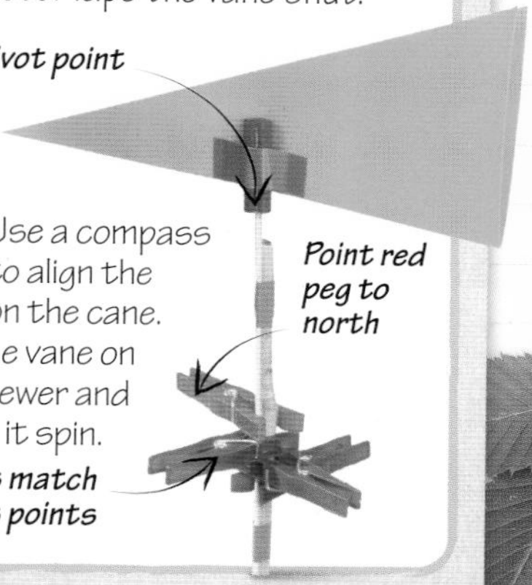

4 Use a compass to align the pegs on the cane. Put the vane on the skewer and watch it spin.

120 Time thunder and lightning

1 MIN

When you see lightning flash, count the seconds until you hear thunder. Sound travels a kilometre every 3 seconds, or a mile every 5, so you can calculate how close the lighting strike was.

121 Identify types of trees

30 MINS

What you need
- *Notebook and pen or pencil*
- *Tree guide – either in book form or online*

There are thousands of different trees in the world, but you can identify the ones in your garden by looking for "marker clues" like a detective. Note them down and consult a guide, and it will tell you what your tree is.

1 First, look at the leaves. Are they long, thin leaves or wider, flat leaves with veins? Trees with needle-like leaves are conifers – evergreens that keep their leaves all year round. Trees with broad, flatter leaves are deciduous – most lose their leaves in the autumn.

2 Conifers like pines have sharp, needle-like leaves, but a cedar has flatter ones. The leaves of deciduous trees can have an alternating or opposite pattern, with one simple leaf or several small leaves on a single stem.

3 Look at the tree's bark – is it smooth or rough? Brown or silver? What about shape – is the tree tall and pointed or does it cast a wide, rounded shadow? Does it have fruit or cones?

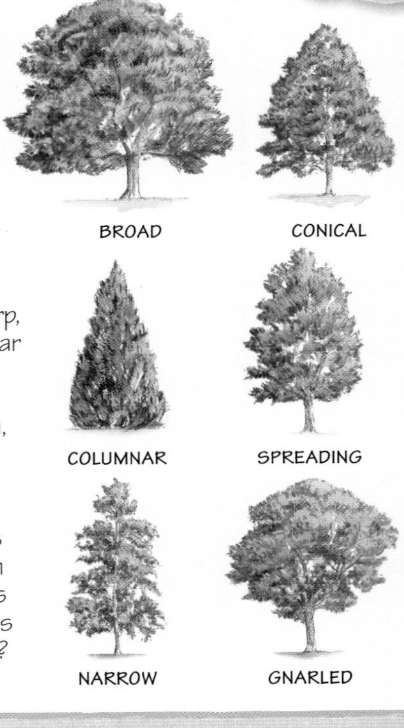

122 Play a game of Poohsticks

5 MINS

Take two sticks, tie grass to one to help identify it, and drop them into flowing water on one side of a bridge. Cross to the other side of the bridge and see which stick comes out first.

Watch the sticks pass by

123 Plant an egg box

10 MINS

Many things we use for one purpose can serve another. The carton that holds your eggs, for instance, is ideal for sowing plants in spring. Give your favourite vegetables a head start. Get planting!

What you need
- Egg cartons
- Seed compost
- Seeds
- Trowel
- Water

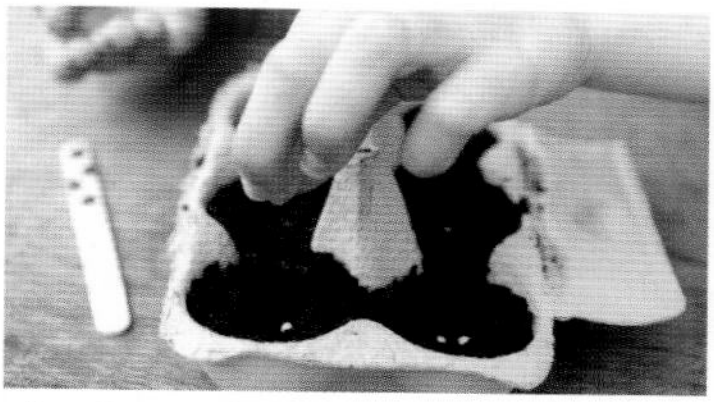

1 Tear off the lid. Fill the carton holes with seed compost. Sprinkle your seeds thinly on top. Cover with compost.

2 Water the seeds gently, then label them. Place the carton on a sunny windowsill. Keep the soil moist, but not wet.

3 When your seedlings sprout, thin out the weaker ones. Once their second set of leaves have formed, the seedlings are ready to transplant.

124 Use toilet rolls as planters

10 MINS

Put toilet roll tubes in a shallow tray, fill each with seed compost. Plant one seed per tube. Keep moist. When the leaves appear, plant in the ground.

125 Train honeybees

30 MINS

Honeybees are especially good at remembering where the best flowers are. When they find new ones, they tell their hive-mates by dancing. Test their memories with some fake flowers.

You will need
- Thin card in five colours
- Scissors
- Water
- Cup
- Sugar
- 5 bottle tops

1 Cut five different coloured flowers out of the card. Mix sugar water in a cup. Put the flowers in the sun, with a bottle top in the centre of each.

2 Put sugar water in one bottle top. The first bees will tell the hive about the food, and other bees will come to the same flower.

3 Take away the sugar water. Bees will return to the same flower, remembering it by sight, even when the food isn't there.

Ask an adult to remove the food – bees can sting you if they get angry.

126 Is it a bee or a wasp?

2 MINS

Bees are covered in fuzzy hairs and have short bodies. Wasps are smooth and streamlined with a narrow waist dividing their thorax and abdomen (body parts).

127 Make a spider's web

45 MINS

Spider webs may feature in horror films, but if you look at them closely, you'll find they're geometric works of art. Try making one yourself and you'll really appreciate just what masters of construction spiders are.

What you need
- *Square of thick cardboard*
- *Small wire ring*
- *Drawing pins*
- *Black yarn*
- *White thread*
- *Scissors*

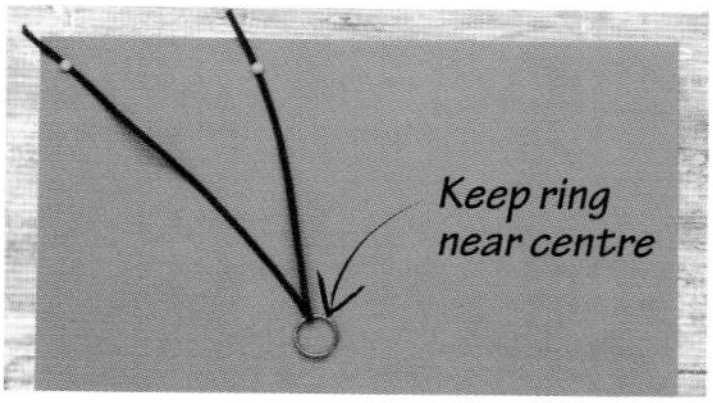

1 Cut six long lengths of yarn. Thread one strand through the ring and pin the ends to the edge. Trim off the excess.

2 Repeat until all the black radial strands are pinned in place and the ring hangs securely in the centre of the square.

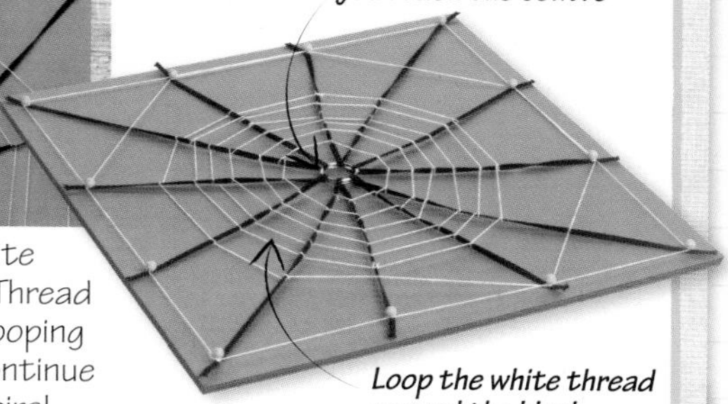

3 Tie one end of the white thread to a side pin. Thread it around the other pins, looping around them as you go. Continue towards the centre in a spiral.

128 Watch a spider make a dragline

5 MINS

Spiders use a dragline, a single strand of silk, to connect themselves to their webs or to steady themselves when jumping through the air. The next time you see a spider, try to spot its dragline.

This line holds the spider steady

129 Create an ice flower mobile

20 MINS

You can make cool biodegradable art that will add to the beauty of your garden – while it lasts. Just freeze some flower heads, leaves, and plant stems in ice and hang them up to enjoy before the Sun comes out.

What you need

• Fancy ice-cube moulds • Thread • Scissors • Flower heads, leaves, twigs • Water

1 Arrange your flowers and plants in each ice-cube pocket. Cut a loop of thread to hang up each cube.

2 Fill the tray, putting a thread loop in each pocket. Freeze the tray for a few hours, then hang up your mobiles.

130 Make an orange pomander

15 MINS

Get that Christmassy smell by making pomanders. Simply stud oranges or mandarins with cloves. Run your fingernail gently over the fruit's skin to release its fragrance.

131 Make a waterfall wall

40 MINS

Recycle plastic containers into this fantastic water wall. Put a bucket at the bottom to catch the water and keep reusing it. Ask an adult to help you drill holes for this project.

What you need
- *Clean plastic bottles and containers*
- *Scissors or craft knife* • *Drill* • *Screws*
- *Wall or fence panel*

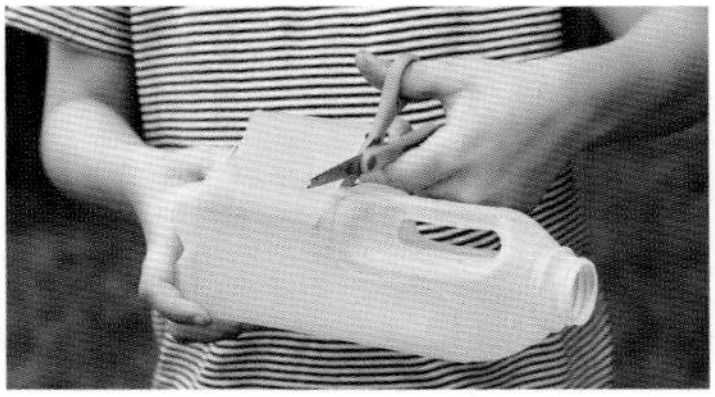

1 Cut holes in the sides of the bottles. These must be large enough to catch the water and to get your hands inside to hold and fix screws to the wall.

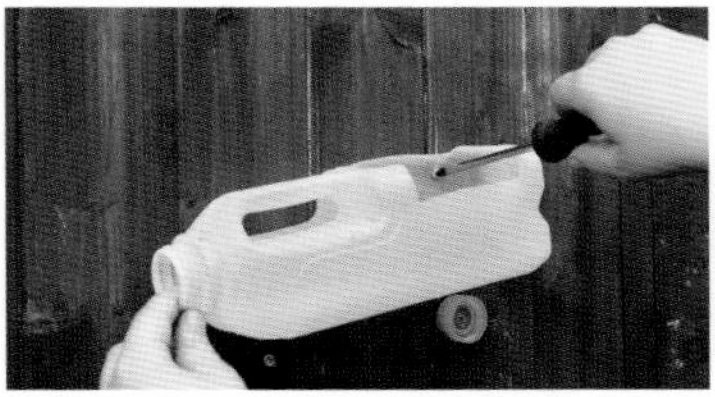

2 Cut a small X into the side, near the hole, then fix a screw through this into the fence. Use two screws per bottle.

3 Tilt the bottles slightly as you fix them to the wall. Test the flow as you go. Put a bucket at the bottom and start the waterfall.

132 Make a waterslide

10 MINS

Lay some partially inflated lilos on the grass. Position the end of a garden hose on them, turn on the water, launch yourself at the lilos, and let the sliding fun begin!

Try running and sliding

133 Build a container pond

40 MINS

What you need
- Clean bricks or gravel
- Container holding at least 40 litres (10½ gal)
- Aquatic plants
- Rainwater

Ponds make great wildlife havens. Even if you only have a balcony, you have space for a mini pond. Put it in a shady place so it won't dry out, and remember to get it into its final position before you fill it with water.

1 Put the bricks in the container bottom to make a platform for the plants. Pour in the gravel. Fill two-thirds full with rainwater.

2 Add plants: oxygen-makers first, then edging plants. Leave the edging plants in pots, but add some gravel to weigh them down.

3 Fill the pond with rainwater. Put one or two floating plants on top. Add a stick bridge so any creatures that fall in can escape.

Stick reaches to edge

134 Let life begin

5 MINS

Fill a jar with rainwater. After a few days, does it turn green? This means microscopic life has begun in your jar. Look closely – you may also see insect larvae swimming around.

135 Build a shelter

15 MINS

What you need
- An old sheet or blanket
- Strong string or twine
- Something to hold down the corners

Shelters come in all shapes and sizes. One of the easiest types to make is a tent held up by one central line. Ask an adult to help you find a place in your garden where you can make this one.

1 Decide where you want your shelter to be. Find two points where you can attach the ends of your central line. A fence post and a tree branch might work, or you could put a hook in the side of a shed.

2 Set up your line, making sure it's not so high off the ground that your tent won't reach. When you're happy with the height, lay your sheet or blanket over the line so that the sides are even.

3 Find something to keep the corners in place, such as bricks, or stones. You could also tap small sticks into the ground and tie the corners to those. Crawl inside and enjoy!

Use your shelter as a hideout or clubhouse

136 Stack a stone tower

5 MINS

Collect a large number of flat stones of different sizes. Start with the largest ones and see how high you can stack them to make a stone tower.

Use smaller stones as the tower grows taller

141 Measure space using your hands

30 MINS

Astronomers describe the size of stars and planets and the distance between them by using degrees. You can use your hand to measure these degrees – "measuring space" as you do so.

What you need
- Your hands
- A starry night

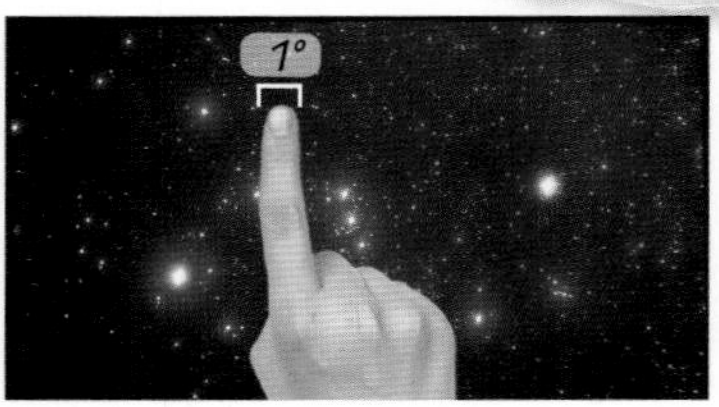

1 Start with your index fingertip. The width of this fingertip, held out at arm's length, is about 1 degree across.

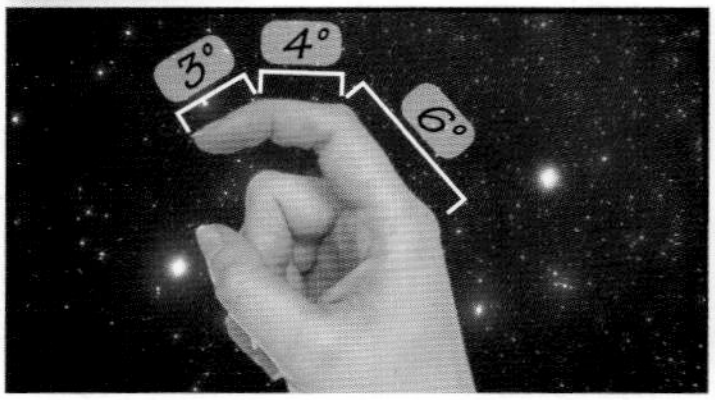

2 Now curve this finger and hold it side-on, still at arm's length. Starting at the top, your three finger joints are equal to roughly 3, 4, and 6 degrees wide.

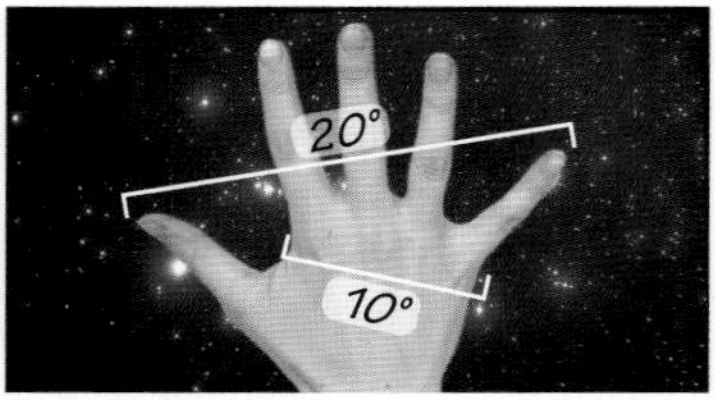

3 Finally, use your entire hand. The measure from your little fingertip to your thumb is about 20 degrees, while the width of your palm is about 10 degrees.

142 Make a moonscape

15 MINS

Fill a baking tray with sand. Smooth it out with a ruler, then drop different round objects into it. Try a grapefruit, marble, ball bearing, or grape. Each represents a "meteor strike" on your moonscape.

Make different sized craters

143 Make a feather collection

20 MINS

Birds come in a variety of shapes and sizes. One of the most striking things about them is their plumage. Some are brightly coloured, others are drab. Discover the wonder of feathers for yourself by starting a collection.

What you need
- *Feathers*
- *Field guide to birds*

1 Try to find clean-looking, whole feathers. Discard any that are broken, have ragged edges, or have chunks missing from them.

2 Use a field guide to identify which species of bird a feather belongs to. Look for clues in terms of colour, stripes, or speckles to help you match the feather to the bird.

3 Try to work out which part of the bird the feather comes from. Long, slender ones are likely to be tail feathers, while small ones with down at the base are body feathers.

144 Unzip a feather

3 MINS

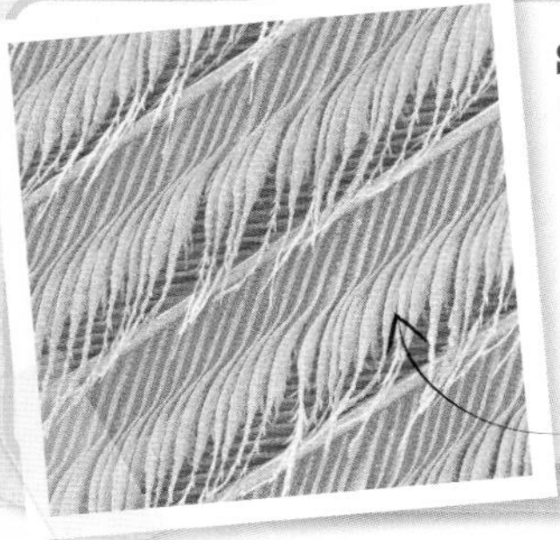

Starting at the tip, run your fingers down a feather to "unzip" it. This makes it looked ragged. Now run your fingers up it from base to tip, "zipping" it back. The barbs in the feather cling together and make it waterproof.

145 Make lavender soap

40 MINS

Some garden plants can have all sorts of uses, including helping us to keep clean. Why not turn some fresh lavender flowers into this perfumed soap?

What you need

- Melt-and-pour soap base
- Plastic mould • Lavender
- Lavender oil • Knife
- Microwaveable bowl
- Mortar and pestle

1 Take the heads off the lavender stalks and grind them into a fine powder with the mortar and pestle.

2 Microwave the soap in a bowl for 40 seconds. Stir in the lavender powder and oil.

3 Pour the mixture into the mould. Sprinkle whole lavender buds on top. Let it set overnight, then chop it into bars.

146 Create a flower perfume

1 HR

Remove the petals and buds from one large rose and three lavender heads. Ask an adult to boil two cups of water in a pan, add the flowers, and simmer for 15 minutes. Leave to cool. Strain into a container.

147 Make a leaf picture frame

45 MINS

Show off a drawing or photograph with a beautiful frame made from leaves and other plant materials gathered in the garden or a park. If you're in a park, only collect items that have fallen to the ground.

What you need
- Leaves, acorns, nutshells
- Pencil
- Cardboard
- Ruler
- Scissors
- Glue
- String
- Tape

1 Place a photo or drawing on a sheet of cardboard and draw around it with a pencil. Use a ruler to draw a smaller rectangle inside. Make sure the edges are wide enough to hold the ornaments. Cut it out.

2 Arrange your items on the frame, then glue them down, and leave to dry. Glue the frame onto your picture, tape a piece of string on either side, and hang up your creation for everyone to see!

148 Make a nature bug

15 MINS

Collect twigs, leaves, and nutshells. Make a body out of clay. Add twigs for legs and antennae and push shells into the body. Use leaves or winged seeds for wings, and berries or stones for eyes.

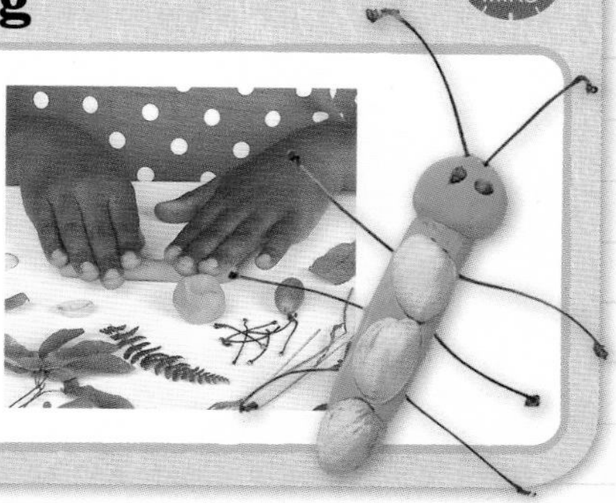

149 Make an erupting volcano

1 HR

What you need
- Plastic bottle • Tray
- Water • Measuring jug
- Food dye • Washing-up liquid • Sand • Funnel
- Bicarbonate of soda • Vinegar

Volcanoes erupt in various ways. Some ooze lava slowly, but others hurl rocks and molten material sky-high. Make this model volcano and watch your very own Vesuvius erupt.

1 Use the jug to measure how much water the bottle holds. Put the empty bottle on the tray.

2 Pile moist sand around the bottle as above. Fill the jug with warm water equal to two-thirds of the bottle. Add two heaped dessertspoons of soda and stir.

"Lava" flowing

3 Add a spoonful each of food dye and washing-up liquid to the jug. Stir. Use the funnel to pour the jug contents into the bottle. Add 100 ml (3½ fl oz) of vinegar to the jug. Pour it into the bottle and stand back. The eruption is about to take place!

It's best to do this outside!

150 Make a stone float

5 MINS

Pumice is a rock made from frothy lava. It contains lots of holes that make it lighter than other rocks. Drop a pumice stone in a bowl of water to see it float. It will sink eventually, as water enters the air holes.

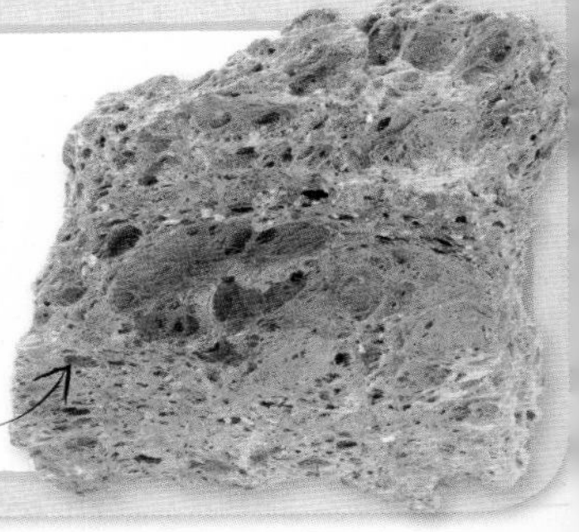

Air holes

151 Build a wormery

1 HR

Earthworms are amazing tunnellers, creating rich compost as they go and adding oxygen and nutrients to the soil. Build this wormery and watch them at work.

What you need
- 3-sided frame, 30 x 20 x 5 cm (12 x 8 x 2 in)
- 2 clear plastic sheets
- 4 bulldog clips • Compost, soil, sand, leaves • Worms

1 Ask an adult to help you make the frame. Cut two sheets of clear plastic the same width as the wood.

2 Glue the sheets to either side of the frame. Secure the ends with the bulldog clips. The clips also give the worm farm stability, so leave them in place.

3 Stand your wormery on a tray. Fill the gap with alternate layers of compost, sand, and soil. Moisten them slightly, then add the worms. Cover them with some leaves.

4 Drape the wormery with a cloth and leave it in a cool, dark place. After a few days, check to see how busy your little wrigglers have been!

152 Is it a head or a tail?

3 MINS

You can tell which end of a worm is which by finding its saddle – a thick band that forms in adult worms. A worm's head is near the saddle. With young worms you have to see which end moves forward.

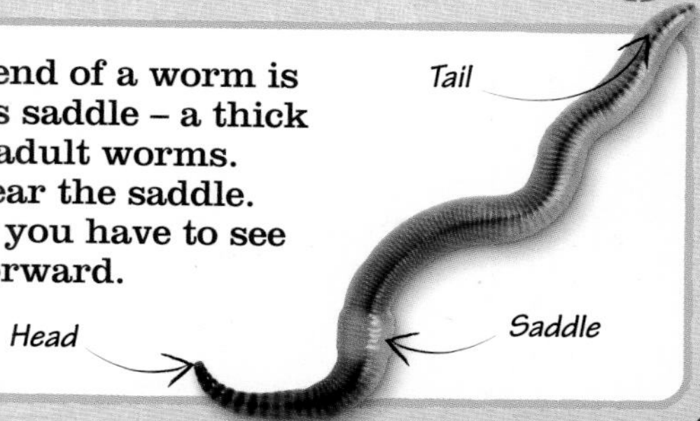

153 Make some conkers

20 MINS

Conkers is an ancient game that has been played in the UK for around 200 years. You only need two players and some horse chestnuts. Try it – it's a knockout game!

What you need
- *Horse chestnuts* • *Glass*
- *Distilled white vinegar*
- *Skewer or bradawl*
- *String or strong thread about 30 cm (12 in) long*

1 Cover the conker with vinegar and soak it for two minutes. (Note: hardening conkers this way may not be allowed, so check first!)

2 Preheat the oven to 250°C (480°F). Bake the conkers for 1½ minutes. Use oven mitts to take them out, and leave to cool.

3 When they're cool enough to handle, pierce each conker. Pull the string through and tie a knot to keep it on. You're now ready to play.

Take care when playing conkers – pieces can fly off when they break.

154 Play a game of conkers

15 MINS

Toss a coin to see who starts. Player one takes three strikes at player two's conker, then hangs his or her conker. Player two then takes a turn. The first conker to break loses.

155 Grow beans on a teepee

20 MINS

What you need
- 4 garden canes
- Wire or string
- Large pot
- Seed compost
- Trowel
- Bean seeds
- Watering can

One of the easiest ways to grow runner beans in a small space is by training them up a pot-plant teepee. It's really easy to do, and you'll be amazed at the harvest your plants produce.

1 Fill a large plant pot with seed compost. Insert four canes into the soil, then tie the ends together in a teepee shape.

2 Make a small hole at the base of each cane with your finger. Plant one bean by each cane. Cover with soil and water well.

3 As your plants grow, guide their stems up the canes. You may need to tie them in loosely with twine to start.

4 Soon your beans will climb up the canes by themselves. Keep them well-watered in dry weather – misting them helps, too!

156 Watch a plant climb

5 MINS

Many plants use tendrils to climb. Look at sweetpeas and you'll see thin, green "fingers" coiled tightly around whatever they touch. Watch how they do this over several days.

161 Play limbo in your garden

45 MINS

Limbo began as a Caribbean dance contest. Today, it's a game of skill as players try to bend over backwards while walking forwards beneath a pole. How low can you go?

What you need
- 3 x 1.5 m (5 ft) canes
- Garden wire
- Wire cutters or scissors
- Friends
- Pencil or pen

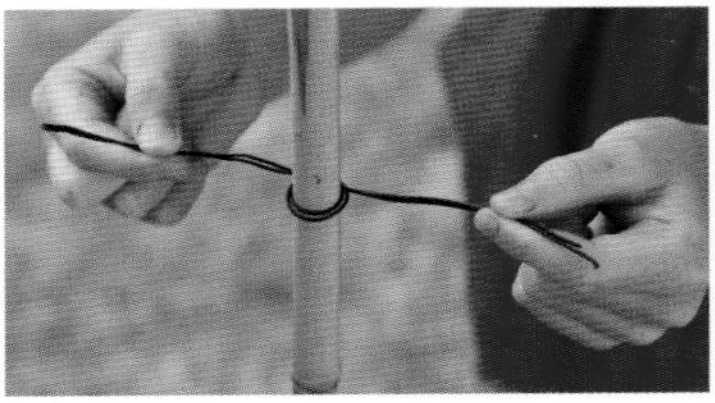

1 Push two canes 15 cm (6 in) into the ground about 1.2 m (4 ft) apart. Mark a point 7 cm (2¾ in) from the top of each.

2 Wrap some wire around the marks, leaving a length to twist into a hook. These will hold the limbo cane.

3 Mark more spaces evenly down the length of each upright cane and add wire hooks to them all. Now you can start the game, moving the limbo cane lower and lower until you find a winner. Put on some Caribbean music to accompany the game if you like.

Don't fall down!

162 Play a game of hoopla

10 MINS

Fill plastic bottles with coloured water. Decide how many points each colour is worth. Set them up with the highest points at the back, toss rings over them, and count up your score.

Try playing sitting or standing

163 Bury a time capsule

1 HR

A time capsule is a collection of items you think would interest people (or yourself) in the future. You can write a letter to the future finder, and include toys, coins, photos – anything you'd be happy to dig up yourself!

What you need

- Sturdy plastic box
- Items to bury – a letter, photos, toy, newspapers, etc.
- Parental permission!

1 Think about what you would like to learn about someone in 50–60 years' time – or longer. Write a letter about yourself.

2 Take a photo of yourself and your family and identify everyone on the back. Include their ages, too.

3 Add some coins minted in the year the capsule is buried, as well as a newspaper listing current world events.

4 Put everything in a sturdy, weatherproof box, seal it, and bury it in the garden for future archaeologists to find.

164 Make a map of your neighbourhood

30 MINS

Draw a map of your local area noting all the places of interest. Are there any big buildings, such as a school or shops. Is there a park or playground? Use a compass to help you position them correctly.

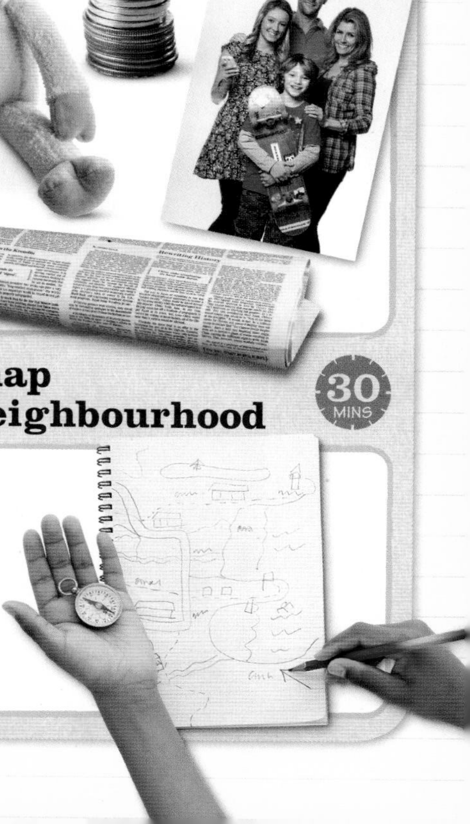

165 Make a bird table

1 HR

Bird tables give birds a safe place to eat, away from predators such as cats. Get an adult to help you build your own bird banquet table and watch them flock in!

What you need

- *Weatherproof plywood cut into: tray: 30 x 40 x 1.5 cm (12 x 16 x ¼ in); tray rim: 1.5 m x 1 cm sq (5 ft x ½ in sq) cut into 2 x 40 cm (16 in) strips and 2 x 26 cm (10 in) strips; post-holder: 50 x 4 cm sq (19 x 1½ in sq); post: 1.5 m x 4 cm sq (5 ft x 1½ in sq)*
- *20 mm (1 in) nails* • *55 mm (2 in) screws* • *Tape measure*
- *Pencil* • *Screwdriver* • *Saw*
- *Hammer* • *Electric drill*

1 Nail the four rim strips to the tray. Leave a gap at each end of the short strips to let rainwater out. Cut the post-holder wood into four pieces.

2 Screw them to the tray base as shown. Saw one end of the post into a point. Push the square end into the post-holder.

3 Drill two holes through the post-holder. Insert screws to fix the post. Hammer the centre of the tray to drive the post into the ground.

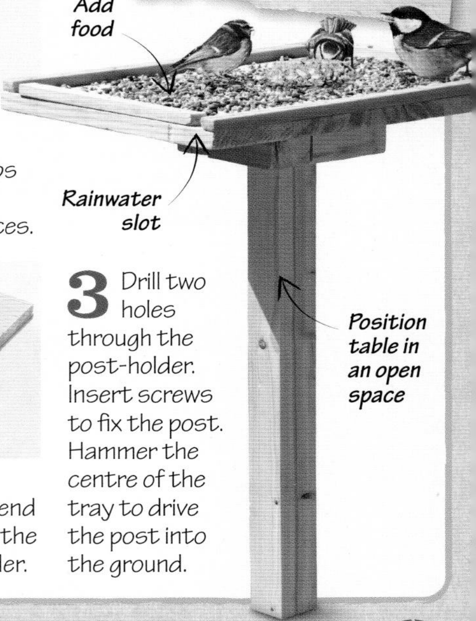

166 Make a ground bird feeder

40 MINS

To make a ground bird feeder, make the tray and rim as in step 1 above. Nail or glue one piece of the post-holder to each tray corner to raise it off the ground. Add a wipeable liner, or pour the seed onto the wooden tray.

167 Paint plant pots

1 HR

Liven up your garden with some bright containers. Add acrylic paint to a terracotta pot and you can show off your plants as well as your artistic skills. Don't forget to weatherproof your designs with a layer of varnish.

What you need
- Terracotta pot
- Acrylic paint
- Glitter • PVA glue
- Paintbrushes
- Clear craft varnish

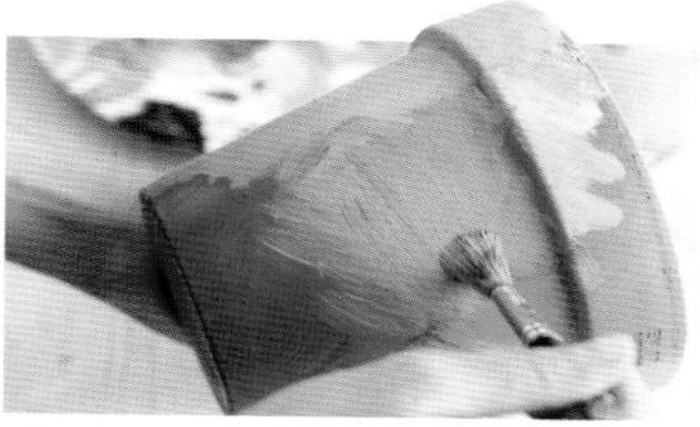

1 Paint the pot with a dark colour towards the bottom. Use lighter shades of the same colour as you move up the pot.

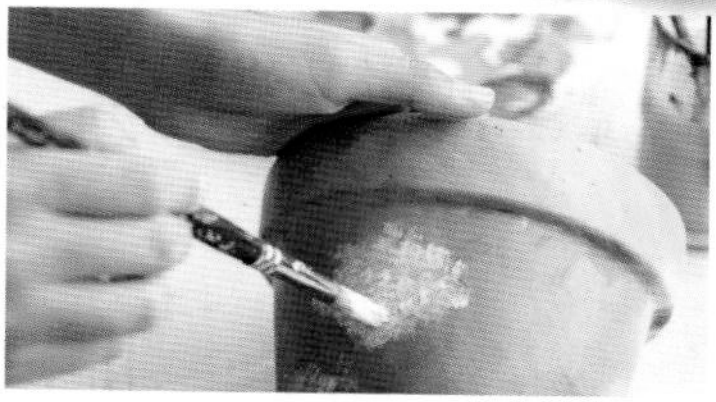

2 When the first coat is dry, add another colour. Here we've put white paint daubs on a blue background to make clouds.

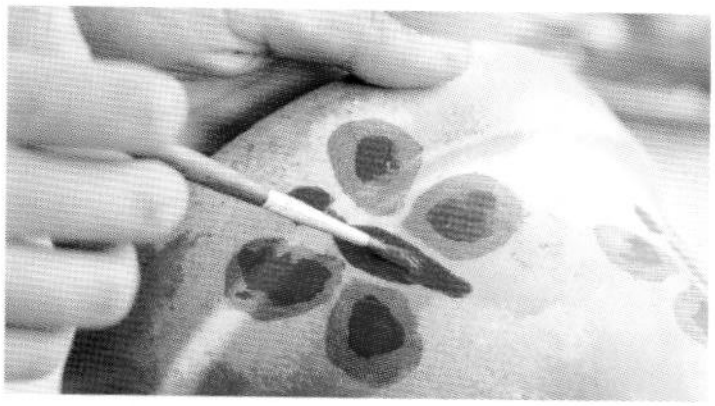

3 When this layer dries, add another. Paint bugs, flowers – anything you like. Paint a shape in glue and sprinkle with glitter. Varnish the pot when it's dry.

168 Make a herb-lined pot

20 MINS

Tie some herbs, such as rosemary, around the outside of a pot or small basket with string. Fill it with flowers as a gift. The herbs stay fragrant for a long time.

169 Make a butterfly net

35 MINS

In spring and summer the air is filled with flying insects. To get a closer look, try catching some with this simple net. Simply wave it over your flowerbeds.

What you need
- 80 cm (32 in) muslin square
- Stapler • Wire hanger
- 60 cm (24 in) stick
- 10 cm (4 in) flexible wire
- Strong tape • Pliers

1 Fold over 6 cm (2¼ in) on one edge of the muslin to make a hem for the hanger to go through. Staple it down along its length.

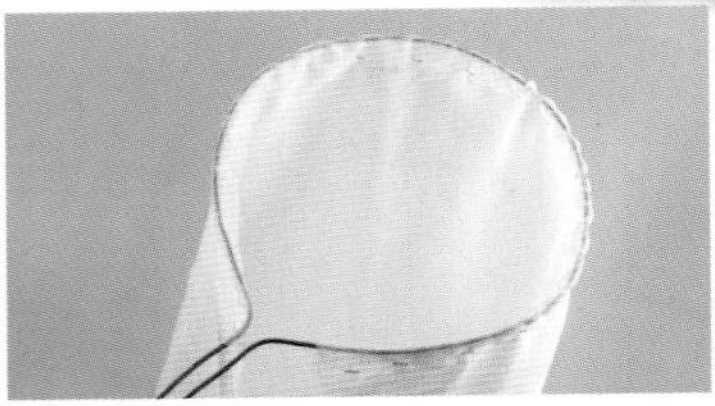

2 Cut off the hanger hook below the twist. Straighten the wire and slide it through the hem. Bend it into a circle, leaving two ends.

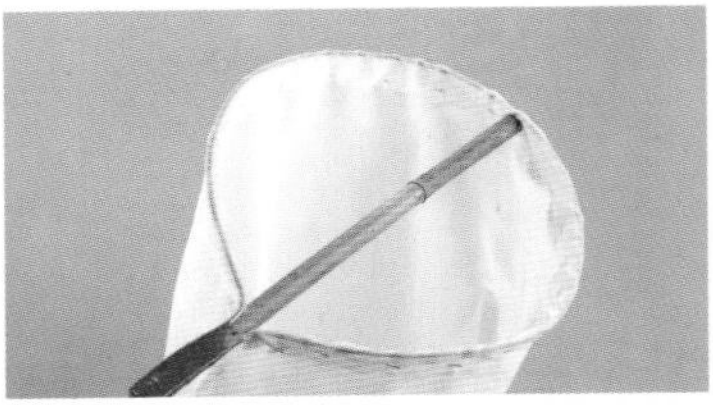

3 Staple together the sides and bottom of the net. Place the stick across the net and tie to the far side with wire. Tape the ends of the hanger to the stick.

170 Is it an insect or a spider?

5 MINS

Insects have six legs, spiders have eight. Insect bodies have three parts: head, thorax, and abdomen. A spider's body usually has two – a head and abdomen. Most insects have wings. Spiders have fanged jaws, insects don't.

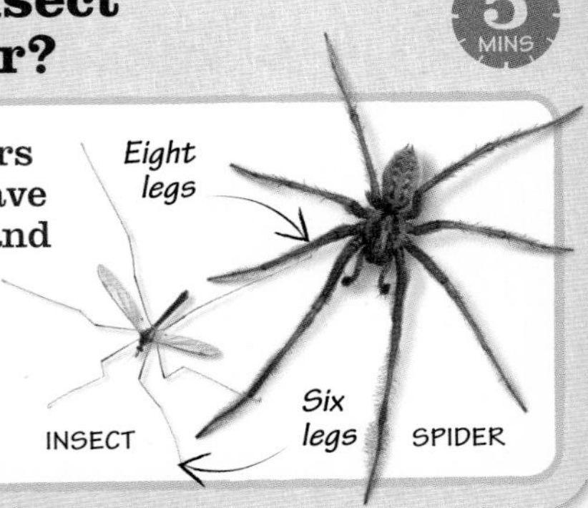

171 Go cloud-spotting

15 MINS

Just like people, clouds come in all shapes and sizes. Some are white and fluffy – like cotton wool. Others are grey and sheet-like. Go cloud-spotting and see how many you can identify.

What you need
- *Your eyes*
- *Clouds*
- *Guide to cloud types*

1 Start by looking at the cloud's shape. Is it puffy and round, spread out in a sheet, or wispy, like smoke? Is it hanging low in the sky or so high you can hardly see it?

172 Forecast the weather

5 MINS

A pine cone can act as a simple barometer. Set it on a shady windowsill. If the scales close, the humidity is high and it might rain. If it's open, the air is dry and the weather will be fine.

177 Make a hanging star

15 MINS

Origami and kirigami are the Japanese arts of paper folding and paper cutting to make decorative objects. Use both of these art forms to make these magical paper stars and light up your back garden.

What you need
- Origami or other coloured paper
- Pencil
- Scissors
- Tape
- Thin ribbon, for hanging

1 Fold the sheet of paper like an accordion. Make a shallow fold at the top, flip the paper, and bend an equal fold back on the first.

2 You should end up with a rectangle. Fold this in half, then make a diagonal 45 degree cut across one corner.

Tape to join

3 Tape the edges of the first star points together. Unfold the star and tape the edges of the last two star points together. Tape ribbon to the back to hang it.

Make a star tree

178 Spot shooting stars

1 HR

Go out on a clear night. Spread a blanket on the ground so you can lie down and look up at the sky. If you see a sudden streak of light, you've probably spotted a shooting star.

179 Draw a treasure map

45 MINS

You don't need to be a pirate to own an ancient-looking treasure map. Age some paper with used tea bags, draw a trail to a treasure (real or imaginary), and you'll have a map that looks hundreds of years old!

What you need
- *Pen*
- *Paper*
- *Used tea bag*
- *Kitchen paper*
- *Cooking oil*

1 First, draw the map on a piece of white paper. Include some identifiable landmarks, compass points, or add riddles and difficult or misleading clues to make the treasure harder to find.

2 When you've finished drawing, tear around the edges of the paper to make it look old – like a real ancient map.

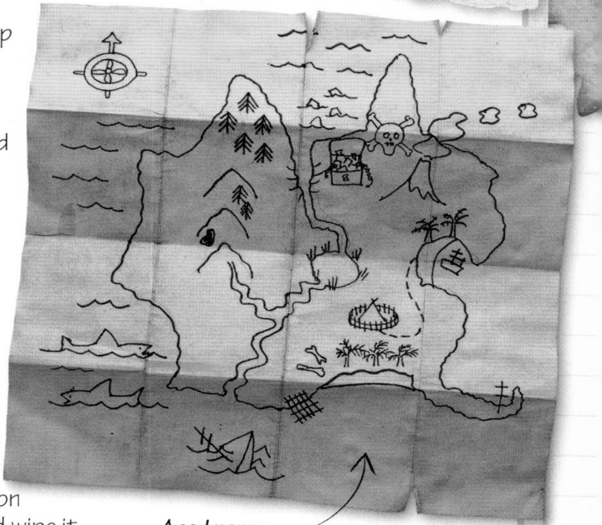

Aged paper

3 Lay the map out on kitchen paper and wipe it all over with a cold used tea bag. The paper will turn a light golden brown. Make sure it's really soaked through, then fold it up and leave it to dry overnight.

4 Carefully open the map. Wipe both sides with some cooking oil, then pat it dry with kitchen paper and let the hunt begin!

180 Go on a treasure hunt

30 MINS

Hide a treasure in your garden – maybe a toy or small box of trinkets. Draw a map to it, or hide clues in various places that lead to other clues. Ask friends to find the treasure.

Tie clues to trees

181 Dig a pond

1 HR

What you need
- Spade
- Waterproof container
- Bricks or stones
- Gravel
- Flat stones
- Water

Big or small, a pond is one of the best things you can put in a garden. It will attract new wildlife and give a boost to any already there. You don't even need a special pond kit – anything that holds water will do.

1 Find a semi-shady spot. Mark out the pond's boundary on the ground with string. Dig a hole the same depth as the container.

2 Put the container in the hole – the top should be level with the ground. Fill in any gaps around it with soil.

3 Put bricks, rock, and gravel into the base to make levels. These will help any creatures that fall in to get out again, so make sure they reach the top.

4 Cover the edges with flat stones. Fill the pond with rainwater if at all possible. If you use tapwater, leave it a few days to settle before adding plants.

182 Plant pond plants

20 MINS

Add plants to your pond to attract wildlife more quickly. You need four types: oxygenators to add air, deep-water plants, floaters, and edging plants. All help keep a pond healthy.

183 Go on an orienteering event

1 HR

If you like treasure hunts, you should love orienteering. The aim of this sport is to use specially drawn maps to find a sequence of flags or points on a set course in the fastest-possible time.

What you need
- *Orienteering map*
- *Compass*
- *Trainers or walking shoes*
- *Comfortable clothes*
- *Waterproof jacket*

1 Find a local orienteering activity near you and sign up for it. It may be a countryside course, but it could also be held in a park in a town or city centre.

Find your way around the map's course

2 Get familiar with orienteering maps. They usually use five colours to stand for different things:
- Black = tall buildings or cliffs
- Brown = landforms, such as gullies or hills
- Blue = water features
- Green = wooded areas
- Yellow = unwooded ones

3 Practise using a compass. Orienteering maps are drawn using magnetic north, so learn how to find north on your compass.

184 Try out your geocaching skills

1 DAY

Take part in a real global treasure hunt. Players use GPS coordinates to lead them to "cached" (hidden) boxes of "treasure" – toys, badges, slips of paper – hidden in the countryside. See www.geocaching.com

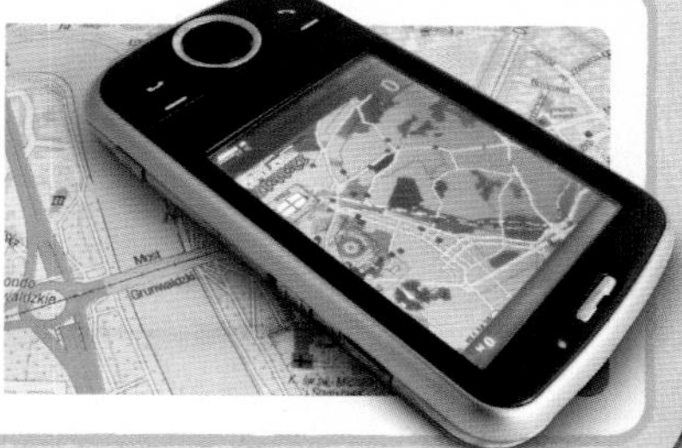

185 Capture animal tracks in sand

20 MINS

What you need
- *Sand*
- *Piece of wood*
- *Dog food*
- *Saucer or small, shallow dish*

When the Sun goes down, creatures that have hidden during the day start to become active. If you want to know what animals come into your garden or backyard at night, set up this easy "track trap" to find out.

1 Cover an area of lawn with sand. Smooth it out with a piece of wood. The sand should be at least 2.5 cm (1 in) deep.

2 Put the dish of dog food in the centre of the sand area, but be careful not to step on the sand, or you'll have to smooth out the surface again.

3 Next morning, check for any tracks. Take pictures or make drawings so you can identify what animal left them behind.

186 Identify animal tracks

10 MINS

You can work out what family your visitor is from by counting the number of toes on the front and hind feet, and whether the claws are visible. The most common are cats, dogs, rodents, and mustelids.

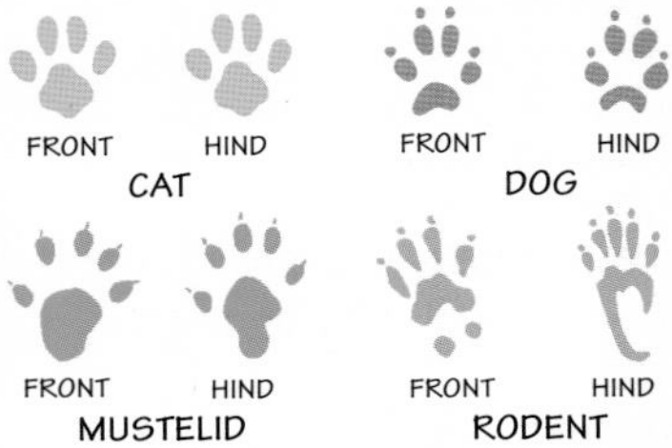

195 Create a woodland terrarium

30 MINS

What you need
- Trowel • 3 plastic bags • Old aquarium
- Small, shallow bowl
- Spray bottle
- Magnifying glass

Woodland trees provide food and shelter for squirrels and deer, but the leaves they lose are home to millions of tiny creatures, such as beetles, spiders, and centipedes. Build a terrarium to find out what lives in your local leaf litter.

1 Use the trowel to put dry and moist leaf litter in one plastic bag. Put soil from other places in the second bag, and bark, small branches, and cones in the third.

2 Spread soil on the aquarium floor and put a half-full bowl of water in one corner. Add some leaf litter, branches, cones, and bark. Spray with water, then put on the lid.

3 Put the terrarium somewhere cool and shady. Spray it every day and top up the water dish. Feed any snails with lettuce leaves. Use the magnifying glass to spot animals. Once you've finished studying the creatures, take them back to where you found them and let them go.

196 Follow an ant trail

5 MINS

Find a nest or put some honey on the ground. Once the ants form a trail, put a leaf across their path. See how long it takes them to go around it.

197 Play pebble dominoes

1 HR

What you need
- 28 flat oval pebbles
- White paint
- Guide to domino game pieces (from the internet)
- A friend

Make a domino set with pebbles and some white paint. Each domino should have a number from zero to six at each end. Paint on all the combinations (6/6, 6/5, 6/4, etc.) to make 28 dominoes in total.

1 Paint the pebbles and let them dry. Put the dominoes face down and mix them up. Let each player draw seven and keep their faces hidden.

2 Whoever has the double-six or the next highest double starts. The next player's domino must have a number to match an open end of the first. If you don't have a matching tile, you miss one turn.

3 Put the tiles end to end to show they match. Once two ends are together, no other tiles can be added to them. Take turns adding dominoes. If you play all seven of your tiles, you win!

198 Make a glow-in-the-dark snake

30 MINS

Collect one large pebble and a lot of smaller ones. Paint them with glow-in-the-dark paint, or decorate them with glow-stickers. Set up your snake with the largest pebble for a head and the rest of the stones for its body. Wait until dark!

199 Make a bubble snake

15 MINS

Blowing one bubble is fun, but what about blowing a whole stream of them at once – one that was as long as your longest breath? See how long a bubble snake you can blow with this easy bubble blower.

What you need
- Clean plastic bottle
- Scissors
- Rubber band
- A dishcloth
- Plastic bowl
- Washing-up liquid

1 Cut off the bottom of the plastic bottle with scissors. Cut the the dishcloth into a circle just larger than the bottle opening.

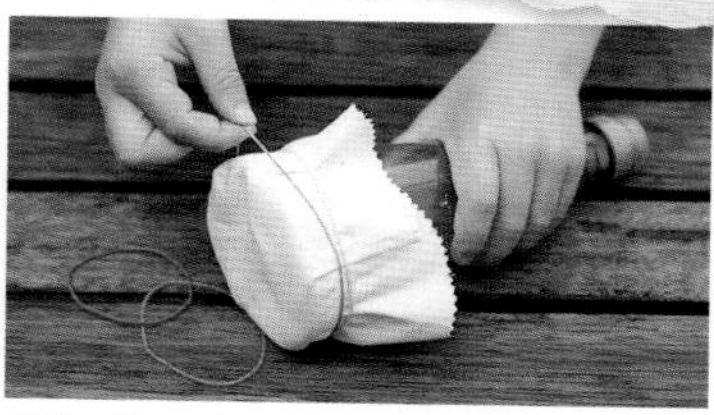

2 Put the dishcloth over the opening and secure it in place with a rubber band.

3 Mix two parts washing-up liquid to one part water in a shallow bowl. Dip the cloth end of the blower, put your mouth to the other end, and blow.

Blow as long as you can!

200 Make a water painting

5 MINS

Take a container of water and sit down at a pavement or patio. Use either your fingers or a paintbrush to "paint" pictures of whatever you like on the dry pavement.

Fingerpaint with water

201 Make a toadstool ring

40 MINS

Turn some leftover plastic toy cases and lolly sticks into some magical toadstools. The painting part is great to do on a rainy day. Make lots and you'll be able to set up your ring outdoors when the Sun shines.

What you need
- Plastic eggshells
- Foil • Egg box
- Lolly sticks
- Acrylic craft paint
- Paintbrushes

1 Put half an eggshell into a long piece of foil. Mould it around the outside of the top to make your toadstool cap.

2 Push a stick inside the foil into the cap. Scrunch the foil around it to hold it in place. Wrap the rest around the stem.

3 Paint the toadstool cap one colour. Let it dry. Paint spots on the cap in another colour. Set it in an egg box to dry. Push the end of the stem into the ground.

202 What's eating your leaf?

2 MINS

Insects that eat plants make tell-tale holes in their leaves. Weevils cut notches out of the edge, while holes in the middle could be slugs or earwigs. Leaf miners make tunnels. Check yours out with a bug guide.

Damage caused by a leaf miner

211 Make your own skittles set

20 MINS

What you need
- 10 small plastic drinks bottles, all the same size
- Food colouring
- Water • Tennis ball

You don't need a special alley to play skittles. Just recycle some plastic bottles, set them up, and use a tennis ball to bowl with. Keep track of the scores and see who's the best skittle player you know!

Try over- and underarm bowling

Add decorations on top – these are worth more points

1 Wash the bottles and remove all labels. Put a few drops of food colouring in each, then fill them up with water. Screw on the lids – make sure they're good and tight.

2 Add decorations on the sides or tops, if you want to – you can make these worth more to knock down if you like.

3 Set up your skittles on level ground in a triangle shape – start with a row of 1, then 2, then 3, then 4. Grab your tennis ball (or any small ball) and get bowling!

212 Play glow-in-the-dark skittles

30 MINS

Put a glow stick in each of 10 clear plastic bottles. Fill them with water and screw the lids on tight. Set them up in a triangle. Use a football to bowl with if the bottles are large.

Activate them first!

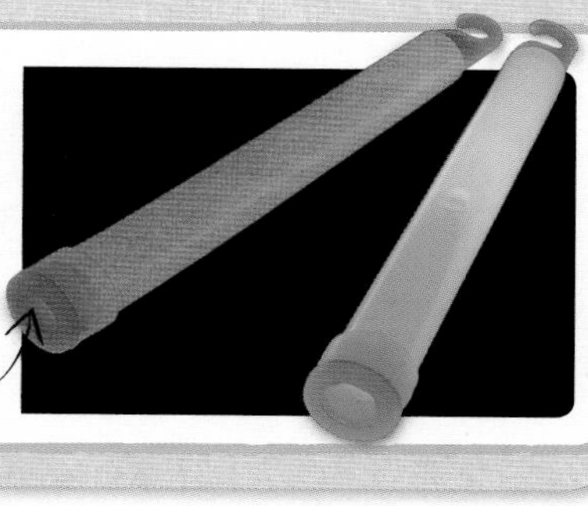

213 Grow your own stalactites

20 MINS

What you need
- 2 glass jars
- Shallow dish
- Spoon
- 2 paperclips
- Hot tap water
- Jug
- 1 m (3 ft) length of yarn
- Bicarbonate of soda

Stalactites form when minerals dissolved in water are left behind as it drips from the moist ceilings of caves. You can grow your own in just a few days with this simple project.

1 Set the jars on either side of the dish. Fold the strand of yarn in half, then fold it in half again. Twist it tightly.

2 Attach a paperclip to each end of the yarn. Put one end in each jar. Move the jars close enough to make a dip in the yarn.

3 Add bicarbonate of soda to a jugful of hot tap water until no more dissolves. This makes a concentrated solution.

4 Pour the solution into both jars, and keep any leftovers to top up as needed. Stalactite crystals will appear in 2–3 days.

214 Tell stalactites from stalagmites

3 MINS

Stalactites hang from the top of caves, while stalagmites form on cave floors. To remember the difference, think of the "c" in stalactite standing for "ceiling" and the "g" in stalagmite standing for "ground".

215 Trap insects in amber

40 MINS

Amber is the fossilized resin of extinct conifers. It often contains the bodies of ancient insects, trapped there thousands of years ago. You can make your own "amber fossil" of an insect overnight.

What you need
- Dead insects
- Pebble
- Plasticine or modelling clay
- Clear modelling resin
- Yellow food dye
- Cocktail stick
- Petroleum jelly

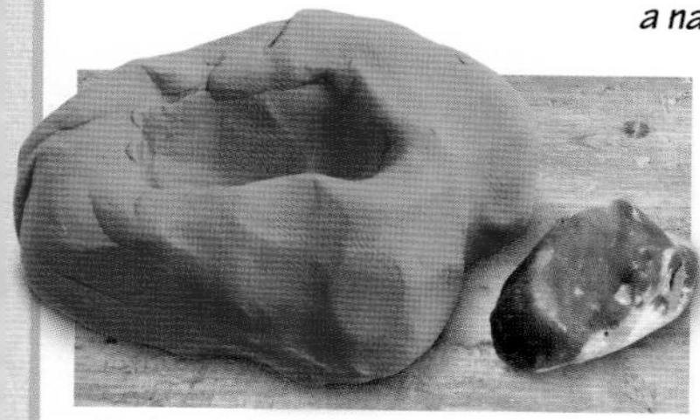

Pebble makes a natural shape

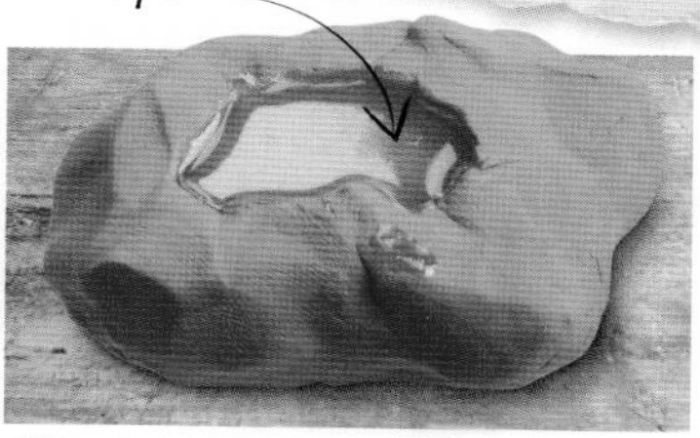

1 Look for dead insects on windowsills indoors or in spider webs outdoors. Press the pebble into the clay. Coat the mould with a little petroleum jelly.

2 Ask an adult to mix the resin – a hardener is usually called for, but just follow the instructions.

3 Add a drop of yellow food dye to the resin, mix well, and pour it into the mould. Drop a dead insect on top and push it very gently into the resin with the cocktail stick. When the resin has dried, wash it in soapy water.

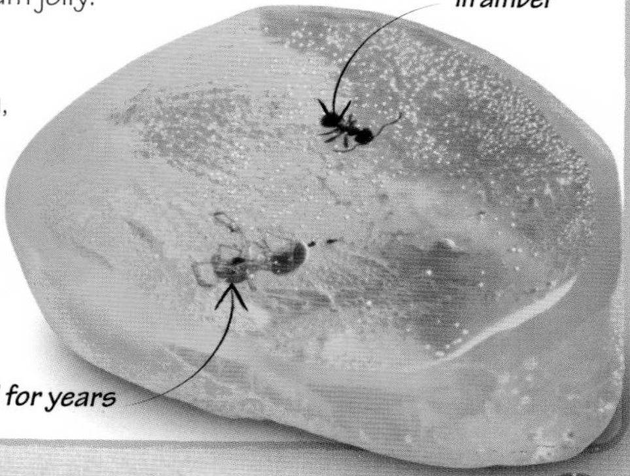

Ants are often found in amber

The insect will be preserved for years

216 Make amber jewellery

20 MINS

Make your amber fossils into necklaces, pendants, or keyrings. Ask an adult to drill a hole in one end to attach a chain or simply attach a jewellery fitting such as a bell cap or bail, to make it look really professional.

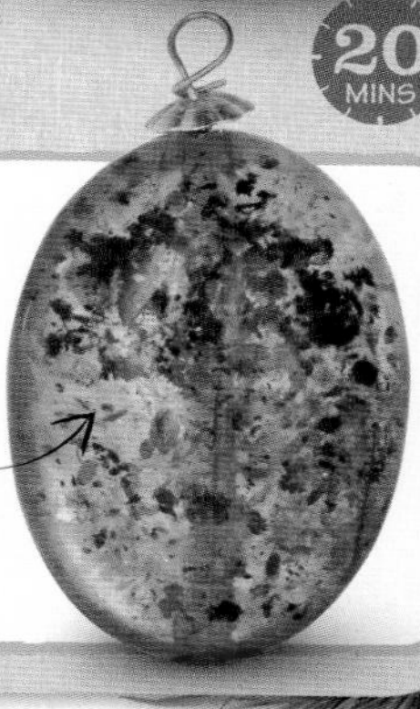

Amber makes a great necklace

217 Make a garden plant label

40 MINS

What you need
• Wooden skewer • Yogurt pots, plastic cartons and spoons, buttons, CDs • Waterproof glue Marker pens • Scissors

It can be hard to tell which plant is which. Making a label will help, and you can make it a lot more fun than a name on a stick. Use these ideas to create some fantastic labels. Just don't forget to add the plant names!

1 For a flower, cut out petals from plastic milk cartons. Glue them to the back of a CD, overlapping slightly as you go.

2 Glue a button in the centre of each petal, and attach a pipe-cleaner centre. Glue the flower to a wooden skewer.

3 Draw faces on spoons with marker pens. Glue on pipe cleaner hair and clothes cut from plastic cartons.

4 For bug labels, cut wings out of a milk carton and glue to a yogurt pot. Add a cork head and pipe-cleaner legs and feelers.

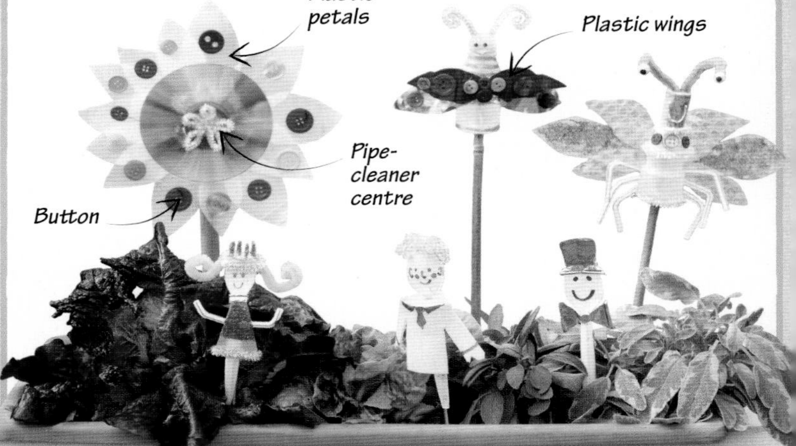

218 Make glow-in-the-dark characters

30 MINS

Collect some smooth pebbles. Glue on string legs and googly eyes. Decorate the body with glow-in-the-dark glue or stickers. When dry, put them in the dark and see them glow.

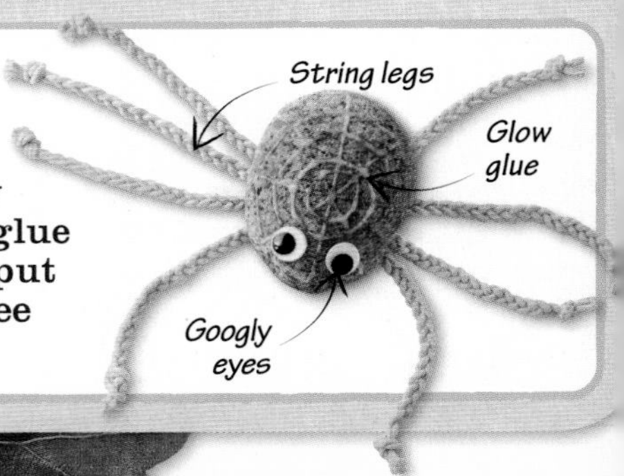

219 Make a peashooter

10 MINS

A peashooter doesn't just shoot peas – it fires any small objects into the air. Make this one to shoot beads, or balls of foil, or paper. Better still, make two and see who can shoot the furthest!

What you need
- Small plastic container
- Balloon
- Scissors
- "Peas": beads, paper balls, or real dried peas

1 Cut the bottom off a small plastic container. Probiotic yogurt drink bottles are ideal – leave the ridged neck on.

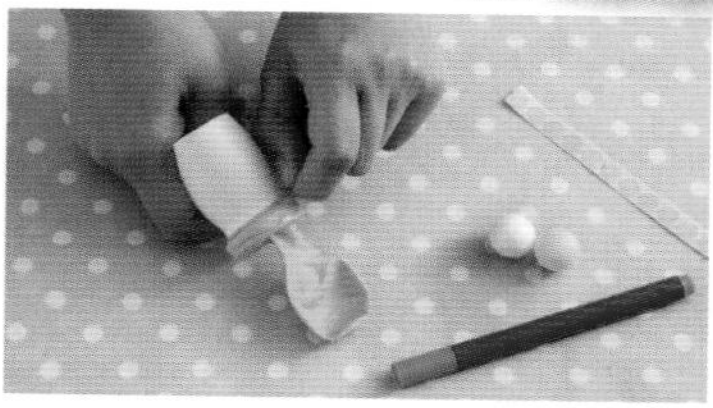

2 Stretch a balloon over the ridged neck of the plastic container. Make sure it's a good, tight fit.

3 Put a "pea" in the cup end. Let it fall into the balloon. Grab the balloon and stretch it back. Aiming it away from people, let go and watch the pea fly!

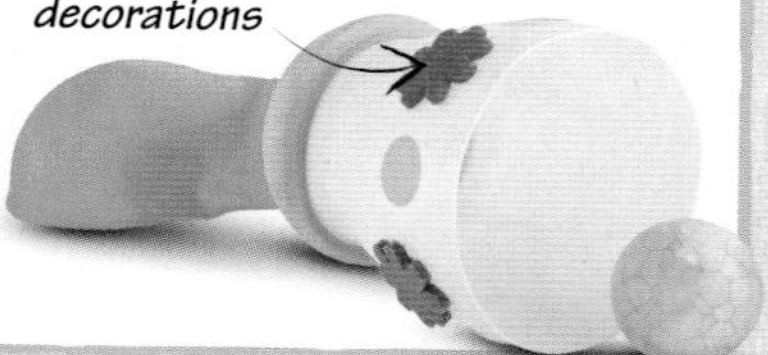

Add decorations

220 Blow a grass trumpet

1 MIN

Pick a clean-looking blade of grass – the wider, the better – and hold it side-on between your thumbs so that it's taut. Blow between your thumbs. The grass vibrates to make a trumpet sound.

Blow in here!

225 Make flower print paper

15 MINS

You don't always need brushes to paint pictures. Collect different kinds of flowers and dip them in paint, then use these natural "paintbrushes" to make some flower prints.

What you need
- Flowers
- Paper sheets
- Poster paint or watercolours
- Small plastic dishes or an artist's palette

Flowers

1 Choose the colours you want and pour a different colour of paint into each dish or section of the artist's palette.

2 Choose a flower head. Dip it into one colour and press it on a sheet of paper. Try different pressures to see what works best.

3 Dip another, different flower head in a different colour to make a pattern with the first flower prints. Once dry, use your printed paper to make cards or wrapping paper – or just frame it as it is!

226 Paint a flower with your hands

5 MINS

Paint your palm with poster paint. Press it on a piece of paper in a circle, like petals of a flower. Try another colour with your other hand.

Press firmly for a good print

227 Lay a stick trail

20 MINS

Tracking is a great skill, and it's easy if you use stick symbols. Grab some friends and head for a nearby park or woodland. Lay a stick trail and see if your friends can find you.

What you need
- Sticks
- 2 watches
- A group of friends
- Let parents know where you're going

1 Agree on your symbols (see the activity below for ideas). Split into two teams – trailblazers and trackers. Be sure each member is with at least one other person and that each team has a watch.

2 Trailblazers should run ahead and lay the trail, using plenty of arrows, especially where the route is overgrown or several paths meet. They should then lie in wait for the trackers.

Stick symbol

3 After 10 minutes, it's time for the trackers to set off after the trailblazers. Time how long it takes for them to find where the trailblazers are hidden.

4 Once the the trailblazers have been found, swap roles and start again to see who's the best at each skill.

228 Memorize some trail symbols

3 MINS

You can make up your own codes, but here are three common ones. An X means "not this way". A straight arrow means "go straight ahead". A dot in a circle means "gone home".

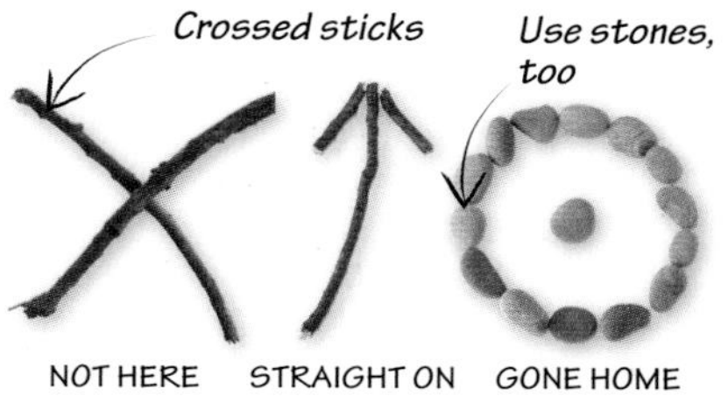

229 Test a plant's senses

45 MINS

What you need
- Lidded shoebox
- Tape
- Matt black paint
- Scissors
- Bean seed
- Cardboard
- Flowerpot
- Paintbrush
- Potting compost

Plants don't have eyes, but they know where the Sun is. Their stems move as they grow towards sunlight, which they need to make food. Put a plant in a box and see how it twists and turns.

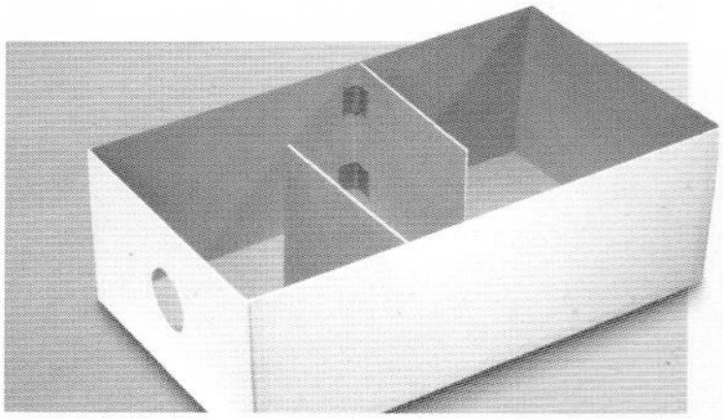

1 Cut out two identical card rectangles as deep as the box and two-thirds as wide. Fix them to the box with tape. Cut a small hole in one end of the box.

2 Paint the inside of the box black. Plant the bean in the pot, stand it in the box (with the hole at the top), and close the lid.

3 Remove the lid every day to see what's happening. The plant will slowly grow around the flaps until it finds the light.

230 Track a sunflower's movement

5 MINS

Plant a sunflower. Note the position of the flower head during the day as it turns from east to west. Plants that follow the Sun are called heliotropes.

231 Take a bark rubbing

5 MINS

Different trees have different types of bark. Some are smooth, some are rough, and some are in between, but all protect trees from injury and disease. Take rubbings to compare the bark of trees in your garden.

What you need
- Crayons
- Thick drawing paper
- Tape
- Field guide to trees (optional)

1 Choose a tree and brush off any loose particles from its bark. Tape a piece of paper to the tree trunk.

2 Rub the paper with the side of the crayon. This will show any unique notches, ridges, and other patterns in the bark.

3 Remove the rubbing carefully from the trunk. Use a guide to identify the tree and write down its name, bark type, and colour.

232 Count tree rings

20 MINS

Find a tree's age by counting its growth rings, the light and dark circles shown in a cross-section of a trunk. One light plus one dark ring equals one full year of growth.

233 Have a picnic

1 HR

Having fun outdoors isn't always about doing things. Being outside makes everyday things special. A picnic, for instance, seems more fun than just plain lunch – so round up some friends and have one!

What you need
- *Food, drinks, and snacks*
- *Paper plates and napkins, plastic drinks glasses*
- *Blanket*
- *Friends*

1 Invite some friends to your house, or arrange to meet them in a park (tell an adult where you intend to go). Ask each of them to bring one or two favourite picnic foods with them to add to the fun.

2 Think about what you'd like to eat. Do you want sandwiches or wraps? Cold chicken legs or sausages? Fruit and salad? Ask an adult to help you decide what would be nice for a sunny day treat.

3 Spread out the picnic blanket on the ground outside. If the grass is damp, put some plastic sheeting underneath it first.

4 When everyone arrives, set out all your food and drink items, pass out the plates, and enjoy your picnic! Don't forget to take all your rubbish home.

234 Pass oranges without using your hands

10 MINS

Tuck an orange underneath your chin – it may take a few tries until you can hold it there. Then try to pass it to your friends without any of you using your hands.

Hold the orange with your chin

243 Make a flower change colour

1 HR

A cut flower uses vessels in its stem to draw water as moisture evaporates from its leaves and head. This experiment shows how this works – and lets you change a flower's colour, too!

What you need
- 2 drinking glasses
- Food dye • Spoon
- Water • Tape
- White carnation
- Craft knife

1 Ask an adult to help. Put the flower on a cutting surface. Slice its stem in two, from the base to halfway up.

2 Tape around the stem just above the top of the cut to prevent splitting. Fill both glasses three-quarters full of water. Add food dye to one glass, stir well.

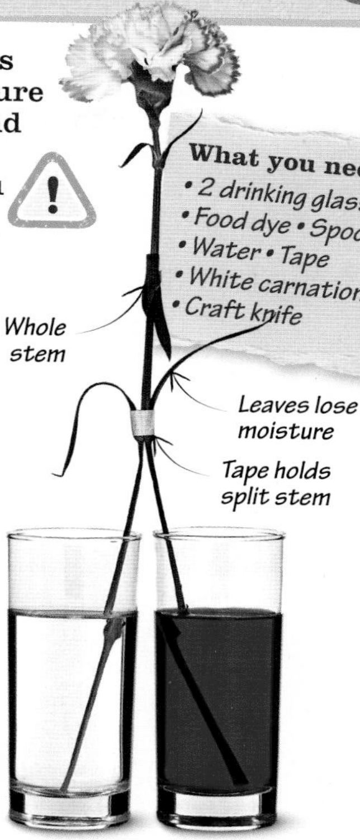

3 Put each half-stem into a glass and lean the flower against a window for support. The flower should start to change colour after half an hour.

244 Arrange flowers in a jam jar

15 MINS

Pick some flowers and arrange them in a bunch, then put a rubber band around the stems to keep them in place. Fill a jam jar with water and put the flowers in. Do several different jars and use them as a centrepiece.

245 Detect small mammals

20 MINS

Many small mammals, such as mice and voles, live secretively in your garden, hiding from predators and humans. You may never spot them, but you can see where they've been!

What you need
- White A4 paper • Scissors • Greaseproof paper • Stapler • Non-toxic poster paint • Long stick • Plastic tube 30 x 7 cm (12 x 3 in) long • Peanut butter

1 Cut two 7 x 4 cm (3 x 1½ in) pieces of greaseproof paper. Staple one piece to each end of the A4 sheet.

2 Mix the paint with an equal amount of oil and brush it on both greaseproof strips. Slide the paper lengthways into the tube.

3 Put peanut butter on the roof of the tube using the stick. Leave the tube out overnight, then check for footprints next morning.

Mouse prints

246 Trace tracks in sand

5 MINS

Gull tracks

When visiting the beach, look for prints in the sand. You may find some small mammal tracks, as well as those made by birds and other creatures.

247 Make a lavender buddy

40 MINS

Hang bunches of lavender up to dry, and after a month you can use the flowers to make a buddy. He may look a little odd, but he'll keep your clothes smelling sweet!

What you need
• Old sock • Uncooked rice • Dried lavender flowers • Stick-on eyes • Fabric scraps • Sewing needle and thread • Pipe cleaners

1 Mix rice with the lavender and fill the sock, twist the end, and sew it closed. Sew on a mouth. Stick the eyes in place.

2 Fold over a scrap of fabric and draw some arms and legs. Cut them out and sew the raw edges together.

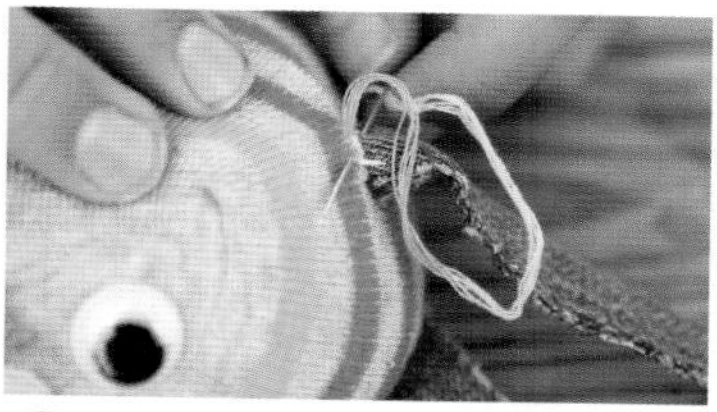

3 Sew the arms and legs to the body. Make "hair" by sewing pipe-cleaners to your buddy's head and bending them into a wacky hairstyle.

248 Hang lavender bag bunting

1 HR

Cut two identical fabric shapes, fill with lavender, and sew them shut. Hang a line of them to keep a room smelling fresh.

Use clothes pegs for hanging

249 Create a desert garden

20 MINS

Not all gardens grow vegetables or flowers. You can make a desert garden filled with pretty succulents – plants that store water in thick, fleshy leaves and stems. Best of all, they won't prickle you like cacti!

What you need
- Trowel • Spoon
- Shallow container
- Gravel • Soil-based potting compost
- Grit • Desert plants

1 Make sure the container has drainage holes in the bottom. Add a thin layer of gravel, then half-fill it with potting compost.

2 Carefully remove the plants from their pots. Plant them, filling in any gaps between them with more compost.

3 Lightly water the plants. Spoon the grit on top of the soil. This helps water drain away from the surface and prevents rot. It also gives a "desert" look.

250 Look for lichens

10 MINS

Lichens are actually an alga and a fungus that live together in places with no soil. Look out for their crusty or string-like shapes on walls, trees, buildings, and rocks.

251 Make a windsock

1 HR

A windsock is used to track which way the wind blows. Make this easy windsock and hang it in your garden. Remember, the opening of the sock points into the wind.

What you need
- Fabric
- Needle and thread
- 76 cm (30 in) long wide and narrow ribbons
- Scissors
- String
- Garden wire

1 Cut a 60 x 25 cm (24 x 10 in) piece of fabric. Hem the short sides. Fold and sew the edge of one long side to feed wire through.

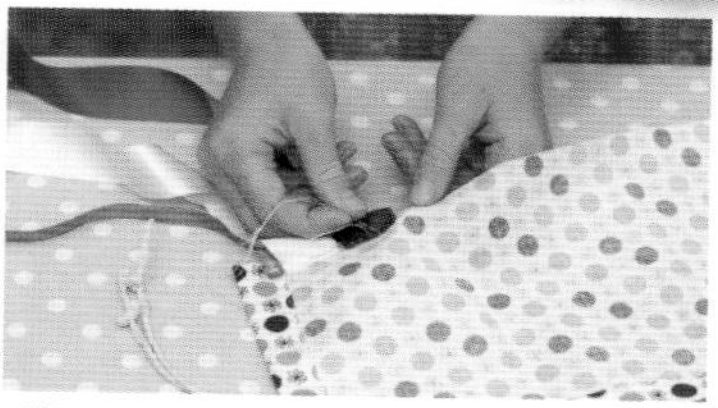

2 Stitch wide and narrow ribbons to the unhemmed long side all along its length.

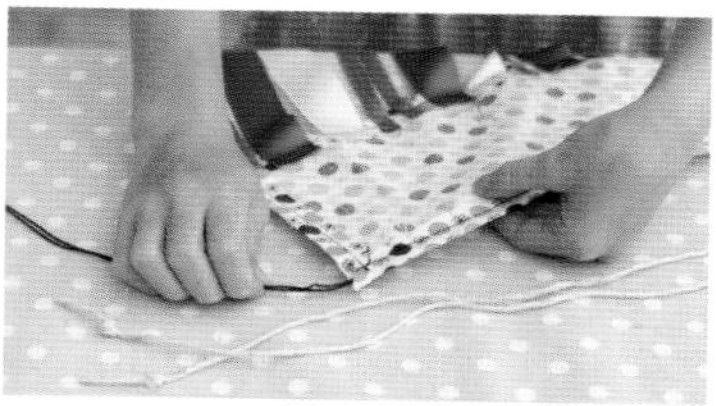

3 Push wire through the long hem. Bend the wire into a circle, twist the ends to join, sew the windsock sides together, then sew on string for hanging.

Windsock droops in slower winds

252 Test which way the wind blows

1 MIN

If you can't see a weather vane, here is an easy way to find the wind's direction. Pick up something light, such as a few fallen leaves, or blades of grass. Toss them up in the air and see which way they go. Do it again to make sure.

253 Make a cloud in a jar

20 MINS

What you need
- *Jar with lid*
- *Aerosol hairspray*
- *50 ml (1½ fl oz) hot water* • *Ice cubes*
- *Blue food colouring*

Three things make clouds – moist, warm air; coolness; and tiny particles in the air that make water vapour condense. This experiment uses hairspray to provide these particles.

1 Fill the jar about a third full of hot water. Swirl it to warm the sides. Add the food colouring. Fill the upturned lid with ice.

2 Leave the ice cubes on top of the jar for a few seconds, then quickly lift it off and squirt in some hairspray.

3 Put the lid back on. You should see a cloud start to form inside the jar. When it fills up the jar completely, take off the lid and watch it escape.

Escaping cloud

254 Find shapes and faces in clouds

5 MINS

Clouds constantly change shape, which is why they're wonderful to look at. Lie on your back and look up at the sky. What shapes or faces can you find?

Heart in the clouds

255 Make a nature mobile

30 MINS

The next time you take a nature walk, why not bring your favourite treasures home and make them into a nature mobile? Once it's done, hang it up where everyone can admire it.

What you need
- Canes • String • Scissors
- Pebbles, cones, fossils, shells, feathers • Vines • Sticks

1 Choose two sticks or canes of the same length. Tie them together to form an X-shape. Make a hanging loop where they cross.

2 Tie objects to the canes with string. Some can be single items, or tie others in chains. Arrange them so that the mobile balances.

3 Try forming vines into loops or stars, or make pine cone animals to hang from the mobile's branches.

256 Play nature noughts and crosses

10 MINS

Lay out four sticks in a grid as shown. Gather two sets of markers, such as pine cones and pebbles, find a friend, and see who can get three in a row first.

Take turns and try to block each other

257 Make a snail racetrack

30 MINS

Even tiny animals make choices, like which way to turn, or how fast to move. Racing snails is a fun way to see how they move as they slide along, leaving slimy trails. Cheer them on as they cross this racetrack.

You will need
- Paint
- Large piece of cardboard
- Pen
- Flowerpot
- Stickers
- Paintbrush
- Garden snails

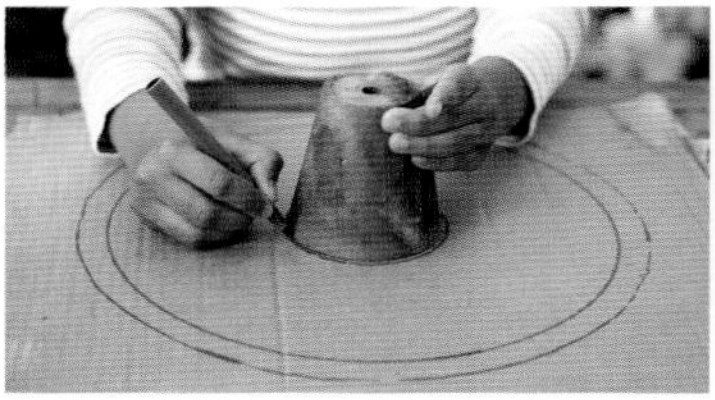

1 Draw at least three different circles on the cardboard, starting with a small one in the middle – use a flowerpot or jar to trace around it.

2 Paint the circles different colours – the centre will be the starting point and the outermost one is the finish line.

3 Number the stickers and put one on each snail. Put the snails in the centre and let them go! Will yours be the winner?

258 Track snails

10 MINS

Put a clay flowerpot upside down outdoors and prop it up on one side. Next day, remove any snails in there and paint a number on each with enamel paint. Put them back under the pot. See which ones return every night.

Cool, dark shelter

259 Sow some seeds

5 MINS

What you need
- Seeds
- Clean yogurt pot or other small container
- Pin
- Seed compost
- Trowel
- Water

Growing plants from seed is like magic – one tiny object holds all the information inside it to make a fully grown plant. Why not sow your favourite seeds in a recycled pot and let the magic begin?

1 Prick some tiny drainage holes in the bottom of the pot with a pin. Fill the pot up with seed compost.

2 Make a small hole with your finger. Pop in the seed to the depth stated on the seed packet and lightly cover it with compost.

3 Gently water the seed – don't soak it too much. Keep it moist. When the seedling shows its first leaves, transplant it into a larger pot or the garden.

The first leaves that emerge from a seed are called cotyledons, or seed leaves. The next pair that form are the true leaves.

260 Have a sunflower-growing competition

5 MINS

Plant sunflower seeds in different pots. Insert canes for support. Put some height marks on each cane and see which plant grows the fastest. Challenge your friends to see who has the tallest plant.

Measure your flowers

261 Create a ladybird sanctuary

15 MINS

What you need
- Corrugated cardboard
- Scissors
- Clean plastic bottle
- Twigs
- Decorations (optional)

Ladybirds eat other bugs that attack plants. One ladybird may eat 5,000 aphids in its lifetime! Invite more of them into your garden by building this cosy place for adult ladybirds to hibernate over winter.

1 Cut the top off the plastic bottle. Cut some cardboard to roughly the same length as the bottle.

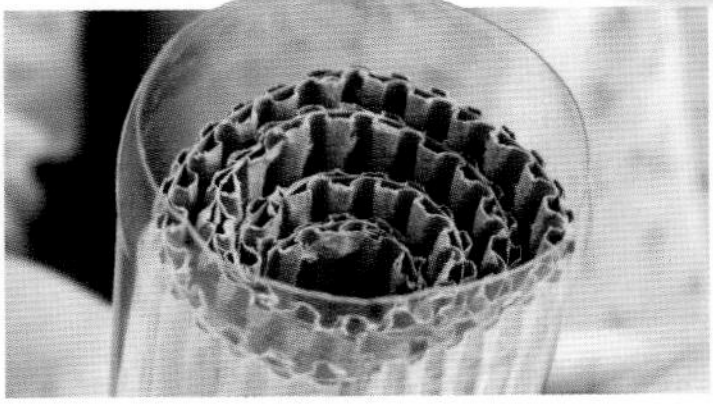

2 Roll up the cardboard as tightly as possible without crushing the ridges and put the roll inside the bottle.

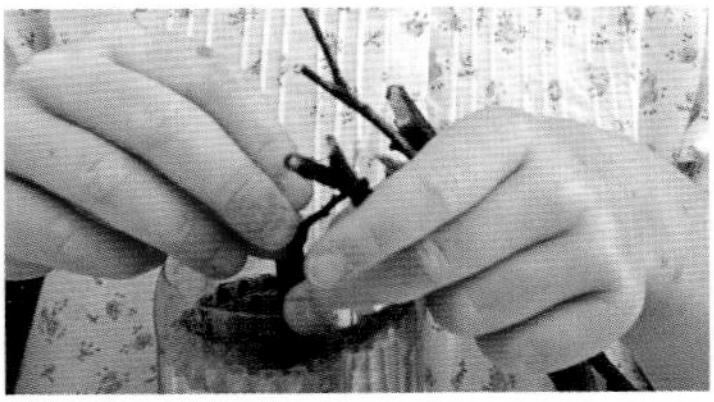

3 Fill the hole in the centre with twigs for the ladybirds to land on. Put the bottle in a bush or other sheltered place. Slope it downwards to keep out the rain.

262 Count the spots on ladybirds

5 MINS

There are about 5,000 species of ladybirds in the world. The seven-spotted ladybird is one of the most common but some have no spots at all. How many types live in your garden?

263 Go pond dipping

1 HR

A pond is a whole world of life in itself, and you can discover it by going pond dipping. Just be sure to handle all the animals you find carefully, and put them back afterwards.

What you need
- Dipping net
- Magnifying glass
- Pond
- Shallow plastic containers

1 Once you arrive at the pond, half-fill your containers with pond water. Then you're ready to put in any finds.

2 Stand at the edge of the pond with your feet firmly balanced on the bank. Try kneeling if this makes dipping easier.

3 Put in your net and move it in a figure-8 motion. Pull it up and turn it inside-out into a container to release your catch.

4 Take a close look at your catch with the magnifying glass. Try dipping at deeper and shallower places for different creatures.

264 Tell minnows and sticklebacks apart

2 MINS

Many small fish are called minnows. You can tell a stickleback apart from them by looking for the spines that give it its name. They lie in a line along its backbone.

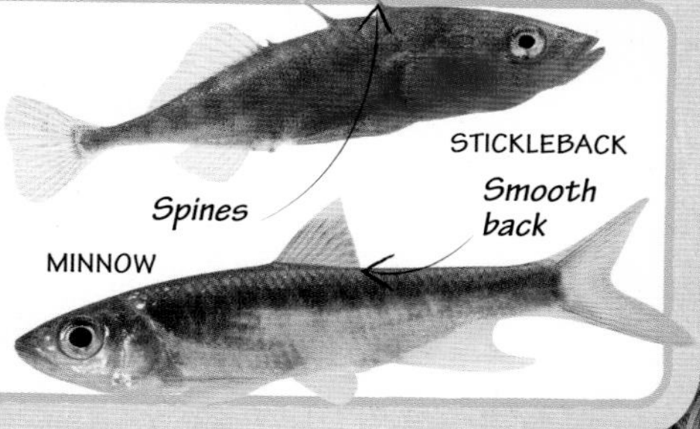

265 Make a tent hideout

40 MINS

Making your own tent is fun – and if you use this design, you can take it apart and store it for use again next year. Simply assemble the two side panels and fix them together. What could be easier?

What you need

- 4 x 1.2 m (4 ft) canes
- 4 x 1.5 m (5 ft) canes
- 4 x 1.8 m (6 ft) canes
- Strong tape • String
- Sheet • Clothes pegs

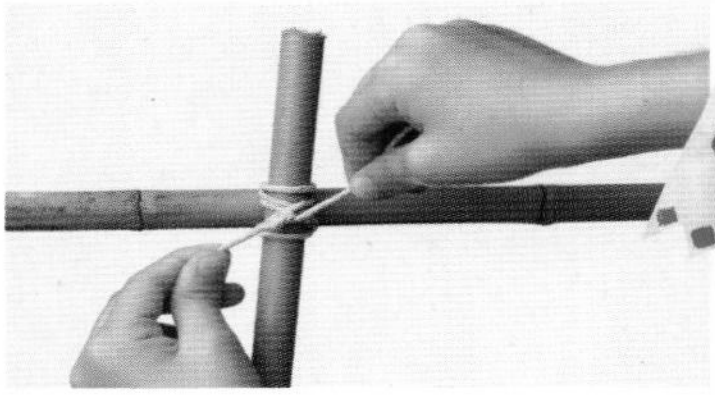

1 Start by using two of the longest canes to form an X for each side panel. Fix these in the middle with tape or string.

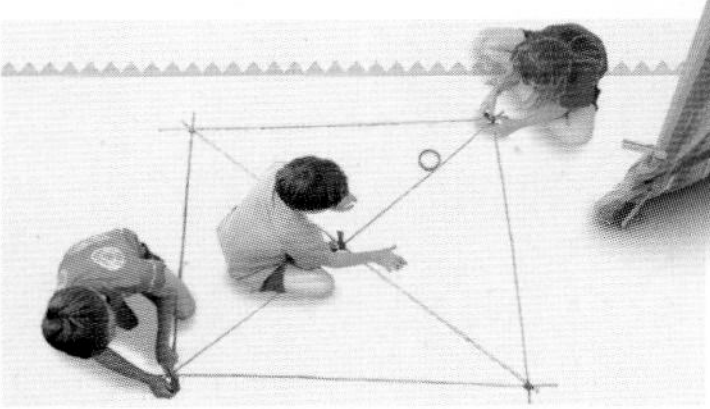

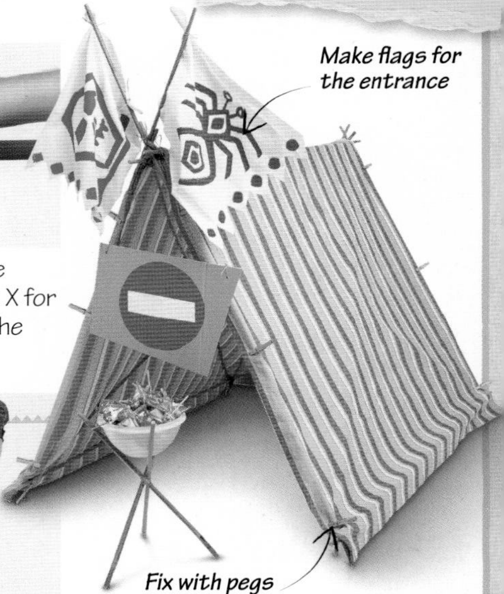

2 Put the next-longest at the top and bottom of the X. Fix these to the X canes, then do the same for the other two sides with the two shortest canes.

3 Ask a friend to hold the sides as you fix the tops together. Make sure the entrance is wide enough! Drape a sheet over the frame and secure it with pegs.

266 Toast marshmallows

10 MINS

Toasting marshmallows on a stick is a fun treat if you're sitting around a campfire or barbecue. Don't hold them too close – they burn quickly. Let them cool before eating.

267 Throw sponge bombs

10 MINS

On a hot day there's nothing better than adding water to your outdoor pursuits. Why not make these easy sponge bombs, put on your bathing suit, then see who can score the most hits?

What you need
- *Large sponges in different colours*
- *Scissors*
- *Hair ties or rubber bands*

1 Cut each sponge into three pieces using scissors. You want two strips from each of three sponges to make a bomb.

2 Hold your six sponge pieces in one hand. Wrap the hair tie twice around the centre so that it's good and tight.

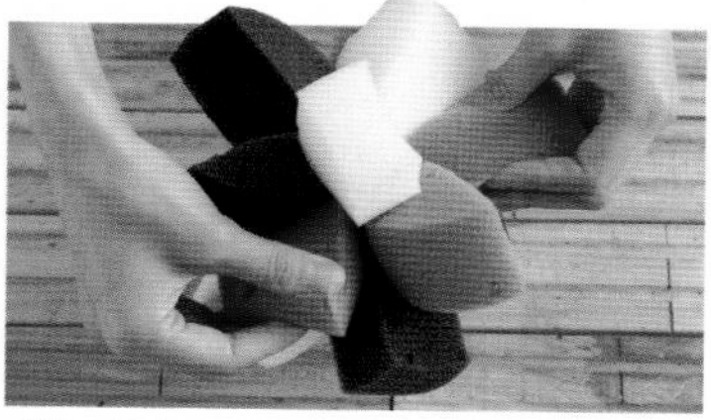

3 Pull the pieces of sponge into shape so that the colours alternate. Then soak the sponge bombs in a bucket of water and let battle commence!

It's a hit!

268 Go wave-hopping

5 MINS

The next time you're at the seaside, pick a smooth, sandy spot in the surf line and jump over the waves as they roll in. Make sure you check how deep the water is before you start!

269 Sketch a bird

30 MINS

What you need
- *Sketchpad or drawing paper*
- *Pencils for drawing and colouring*

Drawing an animal helps you to see it in different ways. Draw a bird, for instance, and you notice things like bill shape, colour, and wing stripes. If you can't get close to a real bird, try drawing one from a photograph.

1 Draw simple ovals – a large one and a smaller one – for the body and head shapes. Add some lines to represent legs, tail, and bill.

2 Look at the size: is it fat or thin? Short- or long-legged? Is the chest plain or speckled? Are its feathers long or short?

3 Study the head. Draw in the colours and patterns around the bill and eyes. Make notes of details to fill in later.

270 Draw a flight path

5 MINS

Fast wing flaps in a straight line are made by short-winged birds like ducks. Slow, steady flappers include herons, while acrobatic flight paths are made by aerial feeders like swallows.

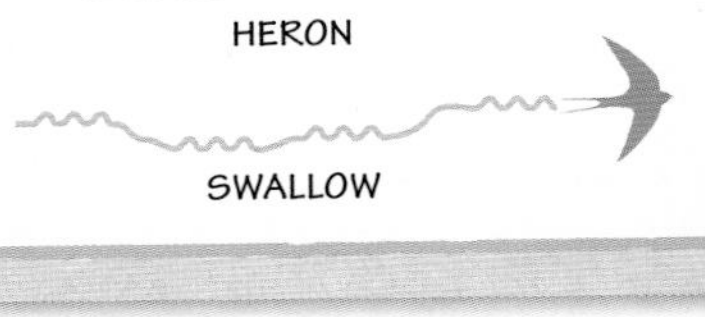

271 Make a spiderweb catcher

15 MINS

What you need
- 3 medium-sized straight sticks
- 1 longer, thicker stick
- String or twine

Some people are afraid of spiders, but they help us by eating insect pests, and are fascinating creatures to watch, especially when spinning intricate webs. You can safely get close to one with this web catcher.

1 Make a triangle shape out of the three sticks, using the string to tie them together at the corners. Ask a friend or adult to help hold them in place to make tying the string easier.

2 Attach the larger stick to the triangle, tying it into place with the string. You have now created a web catcher!

3 In late summer or early autumn, push the long stick of the catcher into the ground, near some shrubbery where you have seen spiders. Check it each morning, and you may find that one of them has spun a web inside the triangle.

272 Identify spider webs

5 MINS

Orb webs stretch across gaps, trapping flying insects. Radial webs have "tripwire" strands that shake the web when touched. Large sheet webs trap crawling or flying bugs.

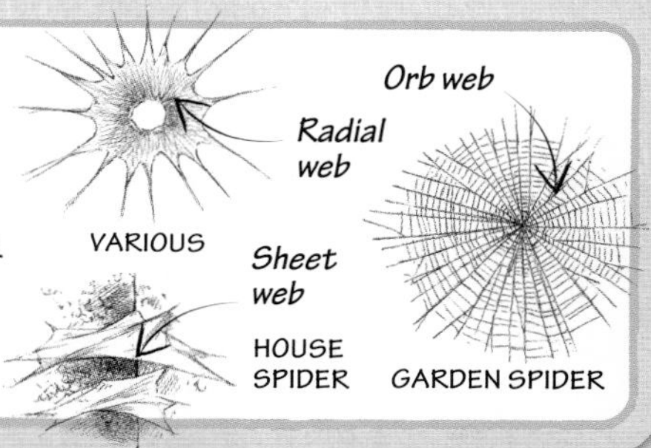

273 Make a leaf collage

20 MINS

What you need
- *Selection of leaves and seeds • White paper • Glue • Stick -on eyes (optional)*

Collages are pictures made using different objects and materials. Coloured leaves are easy to find and use. Try making this leaf turkey picture, then see where your imagination takes you.

1 Lay out your design first to be sure it works, then glue the first leaf onto the paper. Arrange the others like a fan.

2 Once the fan shape – the turkey's tail – is in place, glue another leaf in the centre. This will be the turkey's body.

3 Use a folded leaf on top of the body for breast feathers. Glue on winged seeds for the feet and use a small seed for the bill.

Add eyes to finish the face

274 Create some land art

25 MINS

Designs created outdoors using natural materials are called land art. Why not try making your own? You could use pebbles, cones, or twigs. Remember to take a photo as a record.

Land art sunburst with stick "rays"

275 Make some clothes-peg owls

20 MINS

Most owls don't come out until dusk, but if you have your own, you can enjoy them at any time of day. These little peg owls are easy to make and will look terrific perched around your garden.

What you need
- Thin card
- Scissors
- Pen
- Patterned and plain paper
- Pencil
- Clothes pegs
- Glue
- Stick-on eyes

1 Draw and cut out an owl body from the card. Trace around this on the patterned paper. Cut it out and glue it to the body.

2 Cut out a white face and draw two eye circles. Glue the face to the body. Stick on the eyes.

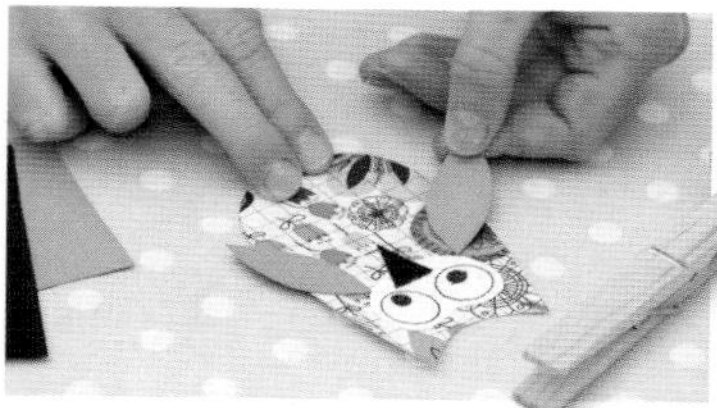

3 Draw and cut out two wings and a beak from coloured paper. Glue these to the owl, let it dry, then glue the owl to a peg. Perch your owl on a twig.

Use plain paper and add dots

276 Hoot like an owl

5 MINS

Clasp your hands together, leaving a hollow. Put your thumbs side by side. Part your thumb knuckles, put your lips over them, and blow.

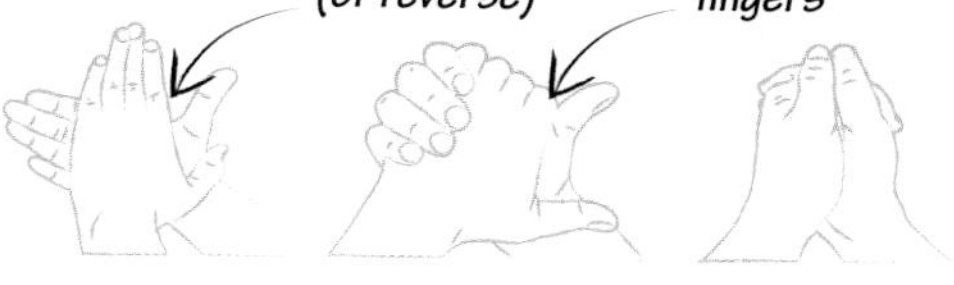

277 Make a sandcastle

1 HR

One of the best things about being at the beach is all the sand – it's an amazing building material. Try it out for yourself by making a sandcastle, as simple or complicated as you want. The only limit is your imagination!

What you need
- *Plastic bucket and spade*
- *A sandy beach*
- *Shells • Driftwood*
- *Other decorations*

1 Find a good place for your castle. It should be far enough from the surf that it won't get washed away, but close enough so you can get water if you need it to wet the sand. Flatten out an area with your hands.

2 Fill a bucket with wet sand. Pack it down tightly, then turn it upside down quickly. Tap the bottom of the bucket gently and lift it off. You should have a tower.

3 Make as many towers as you like in the same way and arrange them in a castle shape. Collect shells, driftwood, even seaweed for decorations, and add a flag on top if you have one.

278 Play a game of beach volleyball

40 MINS

Try to hit the ball back

Divide into teams – you can have one player on each, but two are better. If you don't have a net, draw a line in the sand. Team one serves the ball over the net. Team two has to return it in no more than three hits.

287 Search for soil insects

2 HRS

The soil is teeming with tiny insects, many so small you'd never notice them. With this simple funnel, though, you can discover what bugs live under your feet.

What you need

- Kitchen paper • Wide jar • Soil
- Plastic funnel 15–17 cm (6–7 in) wide • Coarse mesh • Desk lamp

1 Dampen two sheets of kitchen paper, fold them, and put them in the jar base. Crumple some mesh into the funnel.

2 Add some garden soil and shine the lamp over it for 2 hours.

3 The heat from the light will cause bugs in the soil to move through the mesh into the jar. See how many you've collected, then let them go.

288 Distract an ant

20 MINS

Find an ant trail in your garden. Put a sugar cube to one side of the trail. See how long it takes the ants to find the sugar. Try this with different groups of ants to see which finds the bait fastest.

289 Grow a sack of potatoes

15 MINS

What you need

• Seed potatoes • Bin liner with drainage holes, in a hessian or burlap sack • Trowel • Potting compost

You can use containers of all kinds for plants – including bags. Add some soil and you'll even be able to harvest potatoes. You need "chitted" seed potatoes – meaning the eyes have started to produce shoots.

1 Fill the liner a quarter-full with compost. Roll down the bags to soil level. Add three potatoes, eyes-up. Cover thinly with compost, and water.

2 Water whenever the soil looks dry. As they grow, cover the shoots with compost once a month for three months.

3 Unroll the bags as the level rises. After about 90 days, split the side of the bag open and harvest your delicious potatoes.

290 Potato printing

30 MINS

Cut a potato in half. Draw a shape on it with a marker. Get an adult to cut away the flesh with a knife, so the shape is raised. Add paint to a plate, press the shape in it, then stamp it onto paper.

291 Create sunflower people

1 HR

Fill your garden with sunflower people and bring a smile to your borders. Turn paint tins into bodies and pick out a face when the seedheads form for some fantastic friendly plants.

What you need
- *Old paint tins with holes in the base* • *Paint* • *Soil*
- *Marker pens* • *Gravel*
- *Plastic bags with holes in the base* • *Sunflower seeds*

1 Draw or paint "bodies" on the tins. When dry, line with a bag. Add a layer of gravel, then fill with soil. Plant a seed 1 cm (½ in) deep in each, and water.

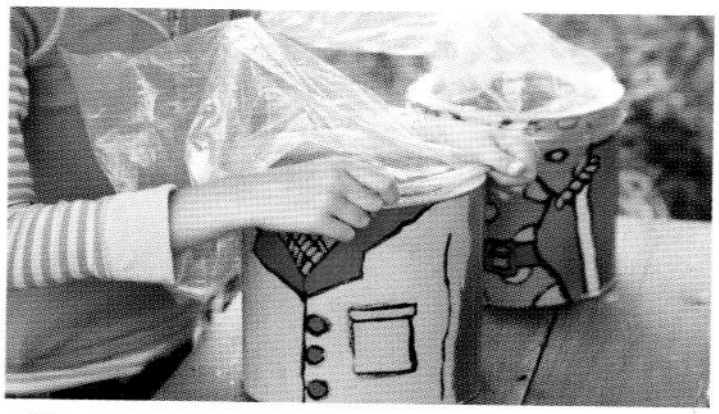

2 Put a plastic bag over each tin, but remove them when leaves appear. When flowers form, remove all except the one at the top.

292 Harvest sunflower seeds

20 MINS

Wait until the petals start to drop and the seeds start to loosen. Cut off the flower heads and rub the seeds with your hand. Dry them before storing.

293 Make sweetcorn husk paper

1 HR

What you need
- Corn husks • Washing soda
- Large stainless-steel pot
- Flour-and-water paste • Old tea towel • Rubber gloves
- Kitchen paper, newspapers

Instead of throwing away the husks from your sweetcorn cobs, use them to make paper that is just like the papyrus used by the ancient Egyptians. Ask an adult to help!

1 Fill a pan with water, stir in 1 tbsp washing soda per litre (34 fl oz) of water. Add the husks and simmer for 30 minutes.

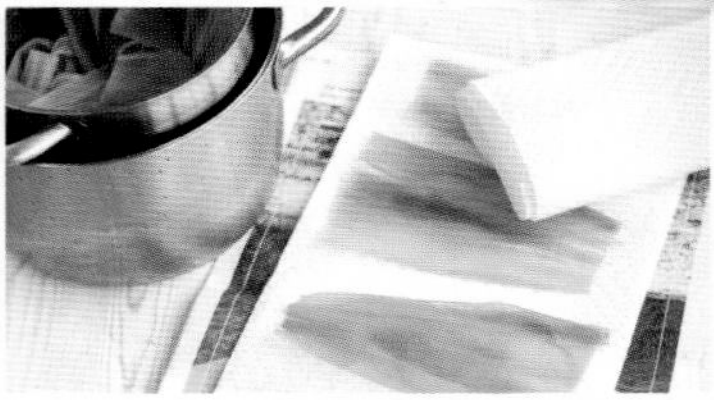

2 Wear rubber gloves. Rinse the husks in cold water. Spread them flat, leave to drain on kitchen paper. Pat them as dry as possible.

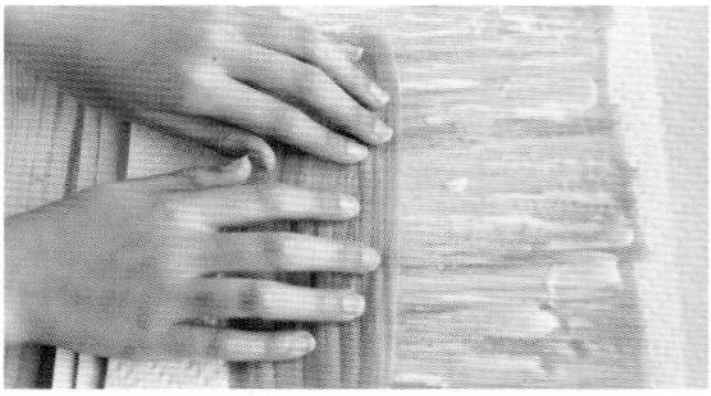

3 Put some husks ridge-side down, overlapping the edges. Brush with flour paste, then put more husks on top, ridge-side up, at right angles to the first.

4 Put an old tea towel on top, then newspaper, and weigh it down with something heavy until dry. Then paint the paper and use it to decorate a notebook.

294 Grow sweetcorn

10 MINS

Fill a container with potting compost. Sow dried sweetcorn kernels 1.5 cm (½ in) deep. Water regularly and leave to sprout for 7–21 days.

295 Catch some tadpoles

20 MINS

You will need
- *Fine-mesh net (like a minnow or aquarium net) • Jar*
- *Plastic container*
- *Magnifying glass*

Tadpoles are the first life stage of frogs and toads. The most common are frog tadpoles, hatched from eggs (spawn) laid in spring. Look for them in nearby ponds or ditches.

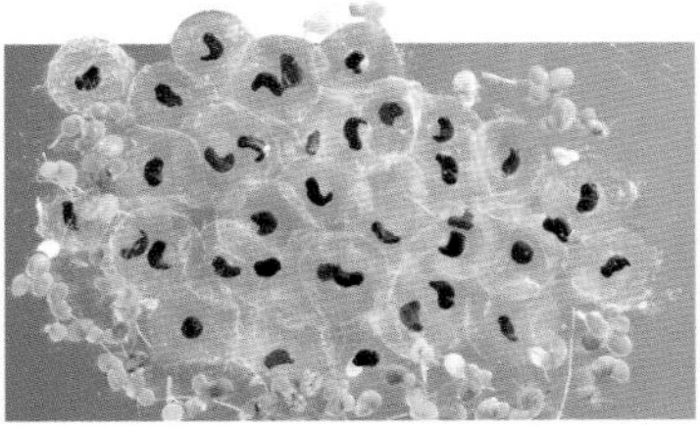

1 Frogspawn appears in early spring. The tadpoles are surrounded by a cloudy jelly, laid in clumps by frogs and in strings by toads.

2 Put some pond water in the jar and container. Look for tadpoles among the water weeds.

3 Put the net in the water under the tadpoles and swiftly lift it up. Quickly put them in the jar, then into the container.

296 How old is your tadpole?

5 MINS

Tadpoles become frogs or toads in around 16 weeks. After six weeks, tiny back legs appear. By nine weeks, the arms start to bud and it looks more like a frog. The tail shrinks to a stump by 12 weeks.

TEN-WEEK-OLD TADPOLE

297 Create a tornado in a glass

15 MINS

Tornadoes form when hot and cold air masses collide and start to rotate, creating a funnel-shaped cloud that causes enormous damage when it hits the ground. Make your own tornado with this easy experiment.

What you need
- Tall drinking glass • Water
- 2 tsps vinegar • Glitter
- 2 tsps washing up liquid
- 2 drops blue food dye

1 Fill the glass ¾ full with water.

2 Add the vinegar, soap, and food dye.

3 Swirl or stir the mixture in a circular motion. Watch the tornado appear. Add some glitter to simulate debris and see how that affects the tornado.

298 Make an ocean in a bottle

10 MINS

Fill a clean plastic bottle half-full with water. Add blue or green food dye and shake well. Top up the bottle with vegetable oil. Screw the cap on tightly. Rock the bottle back and forth and watch the ocean waves roll.

307 Plant a window box

20 MINS

Even if you haven't got any outside space, you can plant a window box garden. Choose plants that flower at different times of year, and you'll always have something pretty to look at. The bees will thank you, too!

What you need
• Window box with drainage holes, plus tray • Gravel • Trowel • Compost • Flowering plants • Watering can

1 Put the box on its tray in your chosen position. Put a thin layer of gravel in the base. Add compost. Take the plants out of the pots.

2 Put in your plants, topping up the soil to their surface level. Fill in any spaces with more compost. Water them well.

308 Make a mini nature reserve

20 MINS

Plant a window box with bee-friendly plants such as lavender, or rosemary and ivy, where insects can shelter. Add a dish of water so tiny creatures can drink or wash in it.

309 Make a foil riverbed

15 MINS

What you need
- *Aluminium foil*
- *Garden hose*
- *Things to float*

You can make your very own "river" in your back garden. All you need is a long length of aluminium foil and some water. Float bottle caps or containers, or make your own nutshell boats (see below) to race.

Have a race with some walnut shell boats

1 Unroll 5 m (16 ft) of aluminium foil. Lay it out flat in the garden or patio (ask permission first) wherever you want your river to flow. Smooth out any bumps underneath. Point the end towards a flower bed or vegetable patch so that the water isn't wasted while you play.

2 Carefully fold up the sides to make walls, about 5 cm (2 in) high. These will form your riverbanks.

3 Put a garden hose at the top and turn it on just at a trickle. Wait for the water to flow. See how many different things you can float down it.

310 Make walnut shell boats

10 MINS

Put a tiny ball of clay in the bottom of walnut shell halves. Carefully push a cocktail stick through a leaf or piece of paper to make a sail. Push the stick into the clay to serve as a mast.

Paper sails

311 Make a pirate ship

40 MINS

Build a pirate ship out of card and a foil container. Once assembled, paint it any colour you like (we chose brown for the bridge) and add sails. Don't forget the skull and crossbones!

What you need
- Clean foil container
- Lolly sticks • Scissors
- Card • Egg box
- Paint • Cork • String
- Wrapping paper • Glue

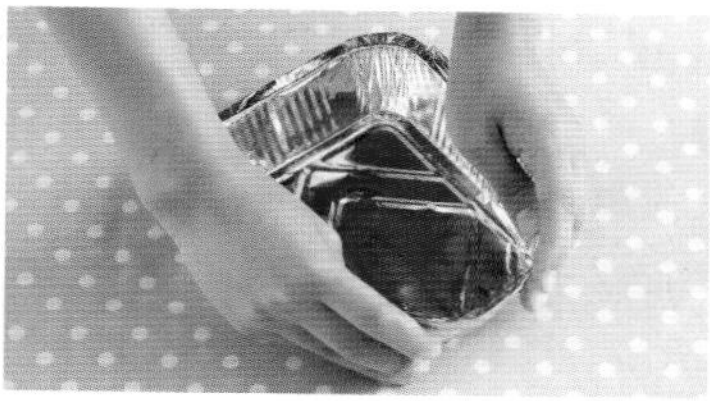

1 Push out the front of the foil container into a point to make the hull shape. Cut a piece of card for the decking.

2 Make cuts around the deck so you can fold it in to fit the hull. Glue it in place.

3 Use the egg box lid to make the bridge. Make two masts out of lolly sticks and glue to the boat. Cut out a wheel from card and glue on a cork for its base.

312 Make a pirate flag

1 HR

Cut out a rectangle of black fabric. Cut a skull and crossbones from white felt and glue it on. Draw eyes, a nose, and a mouth with a black marker. Glue the flag to a cane.

313 Make a fake fossil

40 MINS

What you need
- Plasticine or modelling clay
- Water • Petroleum jelly • Thin card strip • Something to fossilize
- Plaster of Paris • Small plastic container • Yellow or red food dye

Real fossils take millions of years to form, but you can make a real-looking "fossil" in one day with this project. Use a shell, a handprint, a toy, or an actual fossil.

1 Shape some plasticine into a thick, flat disc. Rub petroleum jelly on top. Press your object into the plasticine, then take it out.

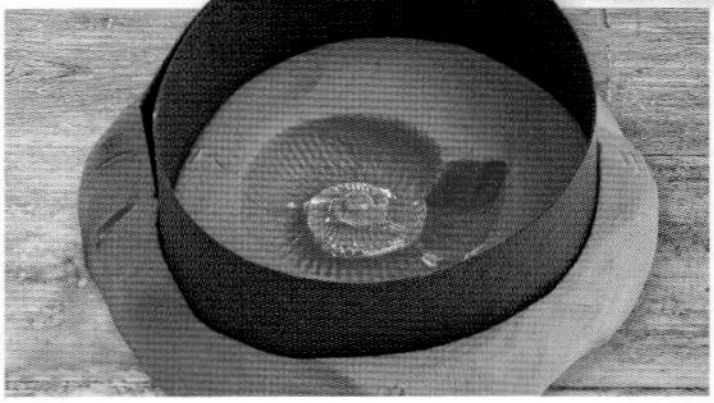

2 Push the card strip into the plasticine around the mould. Mix the plaster and colour it with a few drops of food dye.

3 Let the plaster thicken, then pour it into the mould. Leave it for a day to set. Carefully remove your "fossil". Use it as a paperweight.

A real ammonite was used here

314 Look for shaped stones

10 MINS

Next time you're at a pebbly beach, try finding some shaped stones. Heart shapes are fairly easy to find, but look carefully enough and you may find other familiar shapes.

STONE HEARTS

315 Grow beans in a glass

10 MINS

Roots go down and shoots go up and you don't usually get to watch them do it. Plant beans in a glass, though, and you can see how plants grow. It's a fast, fun way to get your bean plants going.

What you need

- 2 glasses or glass jars
- Kitchen paper
- Bean seeds
- Water

1 Put some bean seeds in a glass, fill it with water, and leave it to soak overnight.

2 Fill another glass with damp kitchen paper. Put the soaked beans midway down the side of the glass.

3 After 2–3 days, the beans should sprout, or "germinate". Remember to keep the paper moist.

316 Plant a bulb in water

5 MINS

Fill a hyacinth glass with water to below the base of the bulb. Put the bulb on top. Place it in a dark place for 8 weeks. Keep topping up the water. When it shoots, bring it into the light.

317 Calculate a tree's height

30 MINS

Have you ever wondered how tall a nearby tree is? Grab a friend and a stick and you can find out. If your measuring tape is too short, just measure in stages and add them up to get the total height.

What you need

- *A straight stick*
- *A friend*
- *Measuring tape*

1 Face the tree. Hold the stick straight out in front of you. Move closer or further away until the stick top is level with the top of the tree, and the trunk base lines up where you're holding the stick.

2 Get your friend to stand by the tree, facing you, so that his or her feet are level with the base of your stick. Turn the stick through a 90 degree angle to your right. The stick base should still be lined up with the tree base.

3 Tell your friend to walk away from the trunk to his left. Stop him when he reaches the end of the stick. Measuring that distance will give you the tree's height.

Hold the stick as level as possible

318 Make a tyre swing

20 MINS

Ask an adult to help you. Find an old tyre and tie a length of strong rope securely around it. Tie the other end to a sturdy branch. Be sure you can reach the swing easily from the ground.

You can sit inside or on top

319 Grow a bug-eating bottle garden

20 MINS

Make an alien mini-world – the plant in the jar is an insect-eating sundew. Put it on a sunny windowsill and watch how any bug that touches its dewy "hairs" gets stuck fast.

What you need
- Aquarium gravel
- Plastic jar
- Glitter
- Carnivorous plant compost
- Sundew
- Plasticine

1 Put a layer of coloured gravel in the jar. Add a layer of compost and press it down gently.

2 Plant the sundew in the compost and firm it in. Scatter gravel on top. Add a plasticine alien. Look out, bugs!

320 Discover a lost world

20 MINS

Fill a tray with a thin layer of gravel, add a thick layer of compost, and plant small ferns and palms. Water them, then add some toys and dinosaurs.

321 Make a pooter

30 MINS

Handling insects can be tricky – some can bite, pinch, or sting. A good way to collect them is by using an insect "pooter". It works by suction, which you provide. But don't worry – you won't swallow any!

What you need
• Glass jar • Plastic tubing • Muslin or gauze • Rubber band • Cardboard • Pencil • Tape • Modelling clay

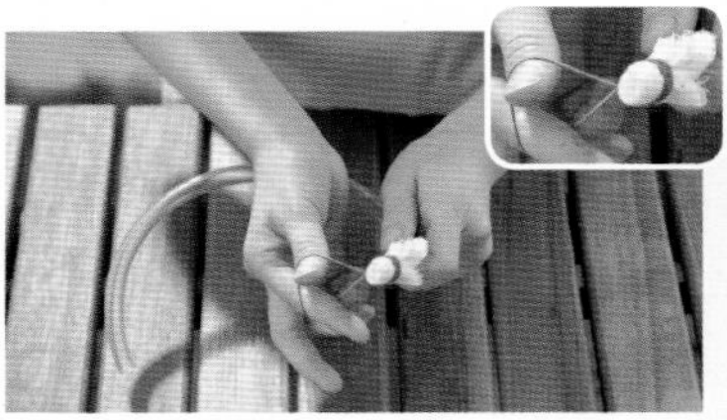

1 Cut two plastic tubes: one 50 cm (20 in) long, one half that. Fix muslin over one end of the shorter tube with the rubber band.

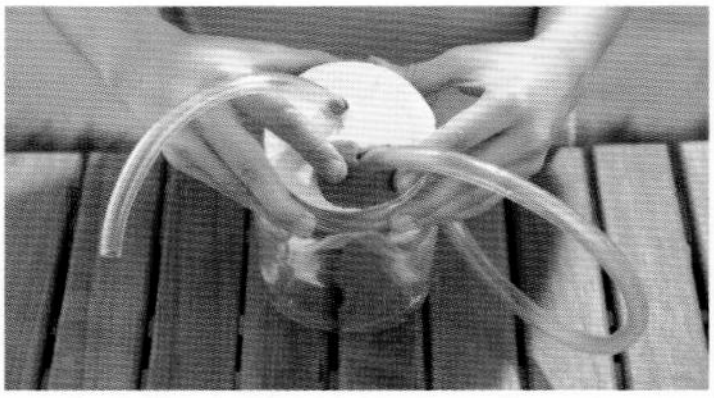

2 Trace around the jar top on card and cut it out. Make two holes, and fix the card to the jar with tape. Push the tubes into the holes and fix with clay.

3 Put the end of the long tube over a bug and suck sharply on the short tube. This will pull the bug into the jar. Study your insect – then let it go.

322 Shake a tree to find bugs

3 MINS

Line a baking tray with some white paper, place it beneath a shrub or tree branch, then give the branch a good shake and see what tumbles out.

323 Put together a naturalist's kit

30 MINS

A naturalist is someone who not only looks carefully at the natural world, but records those observations and learns from them. Why not put together a kit and make your own discoveries?

What you need
• Backpack • Notebook • Pencils • Insect net • Magnifying glass • Binoculars • Tape measure • Penknife

1 Start with a light backpack to carry your essentials. Try to find one with outside pockets for things like water bottles (for you) and collecting bags (for your specimens).

2 Binoculars will help you see faraway creatures such as birds or squirrels, while a magnifying glass takes you into the tiny world of insects.

3 Pack a notebook and pen to write down or draw your observations. A small ruler or tape measure is handy, too, as is a small insect net, but don't forget to use your own senses – they're the most important tools of all.

324 Follow a snail trail

5 MINS

It's easy to find a snail – just look for a silvery, shiny trail of slime on the surface of a leaf, the pavement, or a plant pot. See if you can trace it to the snail itself.

Silvery slime trail

325 Make a windmill flower

20 MINS

Find out which way the wind blows with this bright windmill flower. Add some card leaves to its stem and plant it in a flowerpot.

What you need

- *Thin squares of coloured card*
- *Scissors* • *Double-sided tape*
- *Tape* • *Drawing pins* • *Stick*

1 Make four diagonal cuts almost to the centre. Fold in each corner and stick to the tape.

2 Cut a flower-shaped centre and push a pin through both it and the centre into the stick.

3 Make some leaves and tape them to the stem. Loosen the pin if the windmill doesn't turn.

326 Use CDs to scare crows

15 MINS

To keep birds from eating your plants, punch holes in plastic bottle tops. String them up on canes next to some old CDs and hang them in the garden.

327 Build a bivouac

20 MINS

A bivouac is a shelter or hide made from whatever's available – sticks or branches with ferns or straw to provide cover or help you hide away. Here's one easy way to make your own.

What you need
- 1 long and several shorter branches or sticks
- String, twine, or vines
- Ferns or straw

1 Find a stick that's at least as long as you are tall. Tie two shorter sticks together as shown to support the long stick.

2 Lean other sticks all along the long stick on alternating sides to make a tent-like shape.

3 Cover the bivouac with long grasses, ferns, bracken – anything you can find that will camouflage you and provide shelter. Then try it out for size!

Straw and grass

328 Roll down a hill

1 MIN

Find a grassy hill and have a "rolling down" race. Make sure the ground is dry and free from stones, then lie down and start to roll. See how fast you can go. Who reaches the bottom first? Do things spin when you stop?

329 Force buds to open

20 MINS

What you need
- Twigs
- Jar
- Water
- Secateurs

When trees start to show buds after a long winter, you know that spring is finally on its way. Encourage them to break into leaf a bit sooner by bringing some twigs indoors. Try forsythia, horse chestnut, willow, or birch twigs.

1 Ask an adult to help you cut some twigs with secateurs. Always ask permission first and don't take too much.

2 Make sure the bottoms of the twigs are cut at a slant and place them in a jar of water.

3 Keep the jar in a sunny spot and wait for the buds to open. This could take a few weeks.

330 Look for catkins

30 MINS

Many spring-flowering trees produce their flowers in the form of catkins that appear before the leaves. Take a walk to look for catkins on hazel, birch, willow, or alder trees.

331 Investigate a fallen log

20 MINS

What you need
- Sketchbook
- Pen or pencil
- Digital camera
- Magnifying glass

Nothing is wasted in nature. Look closely at a fallen log, you'll find that it is home to hundreds of tiny creatures – and other plants and fungi as well. Try to disturb this essential habitat as little as possible.

1 Look at the outside of the log. Does it seem like it has been here long or is it newly fallen? Is the bark whole or crumbly?

2 Look closer at the log's surface. Do you see any holes or spider webs? Lift a piece of bark – are there patterns in the wood?

Has an animal made holes in the log?

3 See if there are any signs of animal activity or tracks around it. Note down any plants or animals you find, or take photos to identify later.

Fallen logs are often known as "nurse logs" because they provide a sheltered spot for other seedlings to grow. The rotting material also adds nutrients to the soil.

332 Log your log

20 MINS

Make a log or journal of all the living things you find on or near a fallen log. Revisit your log from time to time to see whether anything has changed. Is something new living there?

CENTIPEDE

FERN

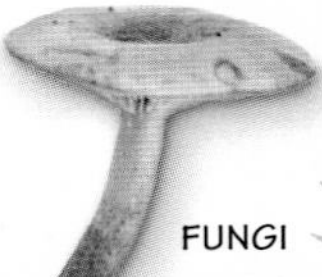

FUNGI

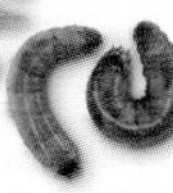

LARVAE

333 Make a nature ice bowl

1 HR

Ice keeps drinks cool, but did you know you can make things out of it? With a couple of kitchen items and some garden flowers, you can make a stunning ice bowl. Use it to serve dessert – or just enjoy it while it lasts!

What you need
- 2 freezer-proof bowls, one smaller than the other
- Jar
- Flowers and leaves
- Tape
- Fork
- Water

1 Fill the large bowl with 2.5 cm (1 in) of water and put it in the freezer until hard. Put the smaller bowl on top. Tape it in place.

2 Fill the space between the bowls with water. Add flowers and leaves, spacing them out with a fork. Freeze for 10 hours.

Try making this bowl with berries and slices of fruit to chill some lemonade!

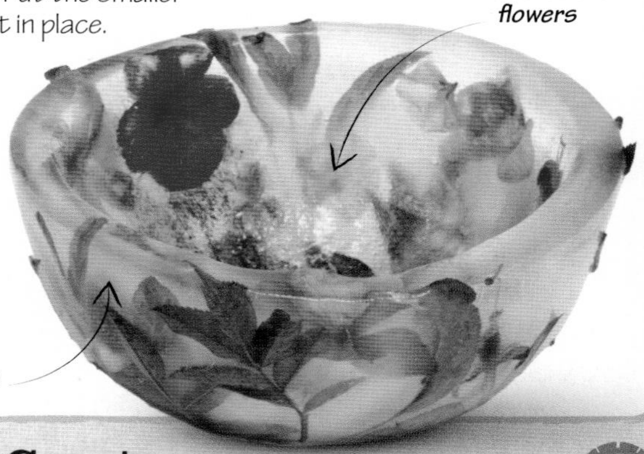

3 Remove the tape and turn the bowls upside down. The ice bowl should slide out, ready to use, and will last for several hours.

334 Create an ice lantern

1 HR

You can make a lantern in the same way using half a plastic bottle as the base and a plastic cup to hollow out the middle. Add leaves, twigs, or ivy, and freeze solid. Turn out the lantern, add a tealight, and enjoy the glow.

335 Keep a Moon diary

30 DAYS

As the Moon circles Earth, it seems to change shape as it moves in and out of Earth's shadow – from a full circle to a thin crescent. Watch the Moon every night for a month, and you can chart all of its phases.

What you need
- Pen
- White and black paper
- Scissors
- Compasses
- Glue
- Aluminium foil
- Binoculars

1 Draw a chart with 29 squares on a large piece of white paper. Cut out 29 black paper circles and stick one in each square.

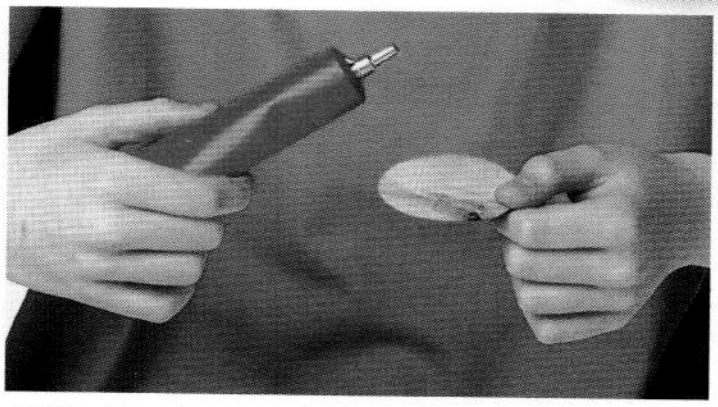

2 Look at the Moon on a clear night. Cut out the Moon's shape in foil and glue it to the first black circle on your chart.

3 Repeat this process every night for one month. Use binoculars if you like, but they aren't essential. If it's cloudy, simply leave that circle blank.

336 Go night walking

1 HR

Take a torch and an adult on a night walk and see what animals you can find. You might see bats or owls, hear crickets calling, or foxes barking.

⚠

337 Make a home for a frog or toad

20 MINS

Toads and frogs like a cool, damp, shallow burrow to hide away in during the day and to hibernate in over winter. Why not make them welcome in your garden by building them a special home?

What you need
- Trowel
- Clay pot
- Damp leaves
- Watering can
- Collected rainwater

1 Find a cool, moist place in the shade. Dig out a hole with a trowel, making the hole a bit longer than the clay pot.

2 Place the pot on its side in the hole. Bury about half of it by filling the inside with moist soil.

3 Use damp leaves to make a nice bed for the frog or toad inside the pot, and water the area to keep the pot in place.

338 Find a frog – or is it a toad?

1 HR

Toads have dry, warty skin, and are usually brown or beige. Frogs have smooth, damp skin that can vary in colour and often have a pale or white neck area.

339 Build a bee hotel

20 MINS

Some bees seek holes in trees or walls to use as nests. The hollow stems of the bamboo in this bee hotel will give them somewhere for their young to grow.

What you need
- *20 pieces of bamboo cane 1 cm (½ in) diameter, 15 cm (6 in) long*
- *Scissors and strong tape*
- *Modelling clay* • *Clay pot*

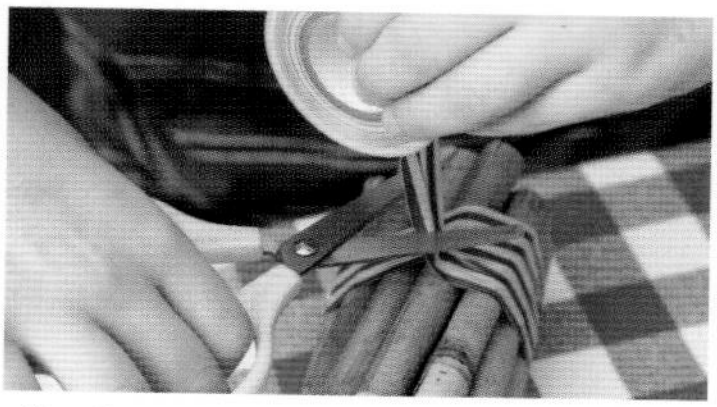

1 Stand the pieces of cane (or hollow plant stems) on end to make a bundle. Use the tape to bind them together.

2 Press the canes firmly into a lump of modelling clay to seal off one end.

3 Put the canes into the pot with the open ends facing outwards. Use some more modelling clay to wedge the bundle tightly inside the pot.

340 Count different types of bee

15 MINS

There are about 20,000 different bee species in the world. Most are solitary types that live alone and don't make honey. Social bees live in colonies. How many species can you spot?

341 Make a stepping stone path

2 DAYS

Make your own stone path by moulding concrete into nature-shaped "stones". Find some really big leaves (rhubarb or sunflowers are good), but ask permission first. !

What you need

- Disposable gloves
- Plant leaves
- Cement mix
- Putty knife
- Large plastic tub
- Sand
- Trowel
- Apron
- Big pieces of cardboard

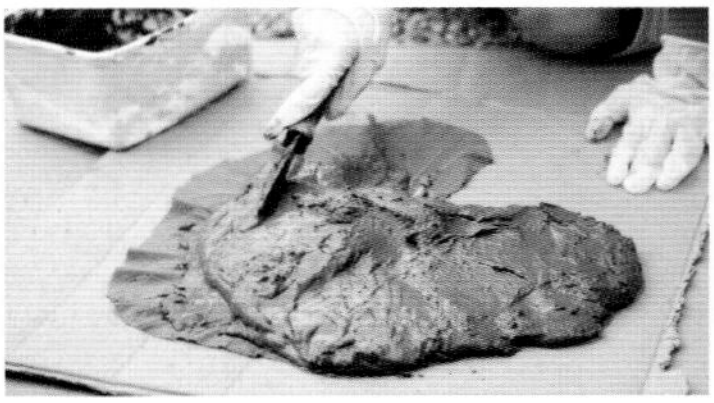

1 Wearing gloves and an apron, mix the cement in the tub. Lay a leaf face-down on the card. Cover with a 4 cm (1½ in) layer of cement, and smooth it over.

2 After two hours, turn the stone over and peel off the leaf. Leave to dry for two days. Arrange the stones into a path.

3 Outline each stone with a trowel, lift, and dig out the soil beneath. Add a thin layer of sand and put the stone on top.

342 Plant a herb path

20 MINS

Liven up a walkway by planting some herbs in gaps between the stones. Choose plants like chamomile for a fragrant path, or colourful herbs for a rainbow effect.

Stone slab

Low-growing herb

343 Test a bird's brain

15 MINS

How smart are birds? Test them with this simple puzzle. Offer tasty treats in two pots – one closed, one open – and you'll find out whether your garden birds are clever enough to work out how to open a lid.

What you need
• 2 identical plastic pots • Card or stiff paper • Pencil • Scissors • Tape • Pebbles • Birdseed

1 Half-fill one pot with pebbles to weigh it down, then top it up with birdseed. You'll do the same with the second pot later.

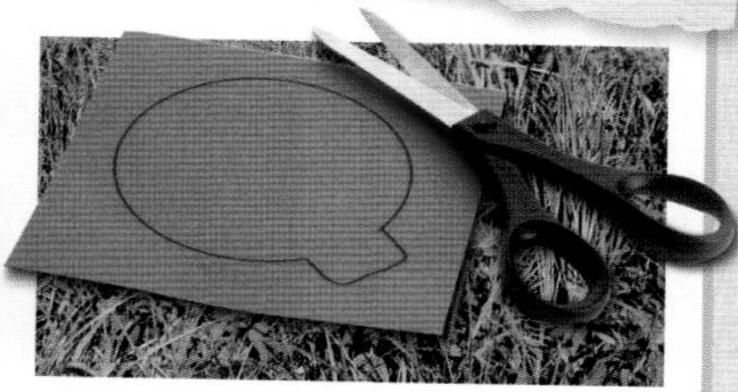

2 Trace around the rim of the second pot onto the card. Cut out the shape, leaving a tab.

3 Fill the second pot like the first. Tape the lid on one side. Put both pots close together. When the open pot is empty, which birds lift the lid to get the seed?

Birds eat from open pot first

344 Identify birdsong

30 MINS

Birdsong tells you which birds are nearby. When you spot a bird singing, make a note of the sounds you hear, and you'll soon learn which one makes which songs.

Use lines to note whether the songs go up or down

345 Make a scarecrow garden buddy

1 HR

This weird, wonderful figure will keep birds away from your plants. Use tins to make his arms and legs, and a plastic bottle for his body. Add a scary face to really put the birds off!

What you need

- Tins, plastic pots, etc.
- Garden wire
- Coathanger
- Glue
- Scissors
- An adult to help!

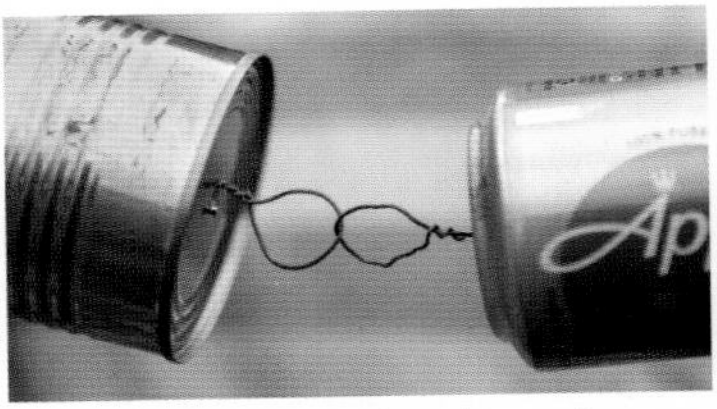

1 Join two tins by threading wire through a hole made in the base. Cross the wires, then twist into loops to join. Make four sets.

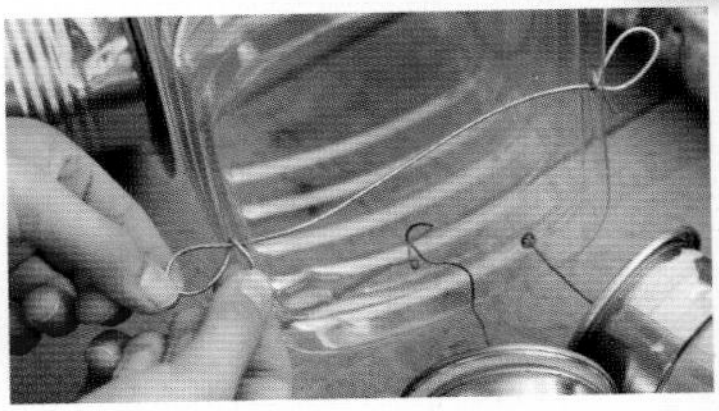

2 Use a plastic bottle for the body. Push two pieces of coathanger through it. Loop the ends and hang a limb off each.

3 Use a plastic pot for the head and glue on bottletops and foil to make a scary face. Wire it to the body, and hang up your buddy.

Add hands and feet

346 Make a traditional scarecrow

45 MINS

Glue on a face

Stuff old clothes full of straw for the limbs and body and tie off the arm and leg ends with string. Stuff a pillowcase for the head. Mount on a wooden pole frame and add a hat!

347 Make a wind chime

40 MINS

A garden isn't just about plants – it should appeal to all your senses, including hearing. This easy wind chime will make a gentle, soothing "tink tink" whenever the wind blows. You probably already have all you need to create it.

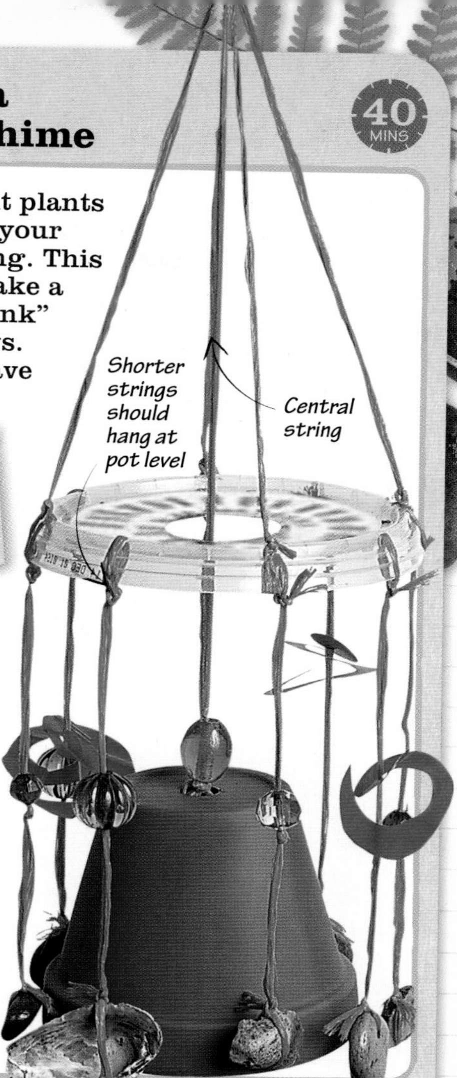

What you need

- *Terracotta pot with drainage hole*
- *String* • *Plastic container lid*
- *Beads, small pebbles, or shells*

1 Tie a long piece of string to a branch. Cut a large hole in the centre of the container lid, and eight holes around the edge. Tie a shorter string to each hole.

2 Thread the long string through the lid and the pot. Attach a bead big enough to block the hole in the pot.

3 Knot four lid strings to the central string to hang the lid above the pot. Tie a pebble, bead, or shell to the ends of the other four lid strings.

348 Paint a pebble paperweight

30 MINS

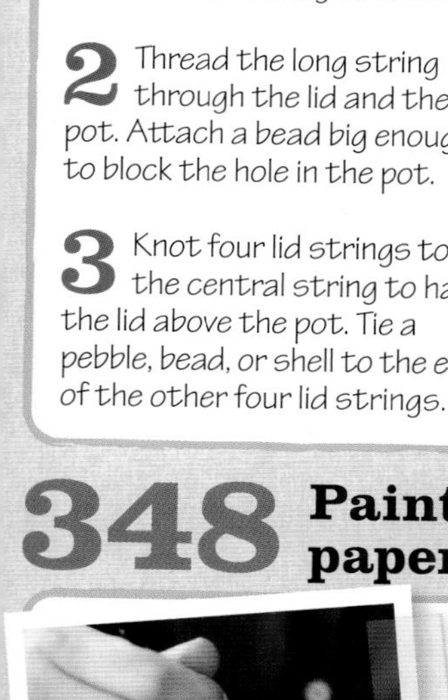

Choose a smooth pebble the size you want your paperweight. Paint it all over in a background colour. When it dries, mark out your design with a pencil or chalk, then fill in the colours.

Dotted design

353 Go beachcombing

1 HR

You never know what you'll find on a beach. One day it could be a whole scallop shell, another day you could find fossils. Go on a beach walk and see what the tide has brought in for you.

What you need
- Sunglasses
- Beach footwear
- Beach bucket or a bag to hold your finds

1 Get started early – the best finds go to the first people on the beach.

2 Look along the tide line, but also check further back. Sometimes the wind blows perfect shells away from the surf.

3 Get your feet wet. You can find great shells in the surf. Also try hunting after a storm when the tide is out.

4 Take only what you really want and can carry easily. Don't disturb any live creatures, and take any litter home.

354 Make a sand face

10 MINS

Use the beach as your artist's palette and make a face out of sand, shells, pebbles, driftwood, or anything else you can find. Or simply draw one in the sand with a stick. Make it as big as you like – the tide will tidy it away.

355 Make a compost heap

40 MINS

Left to itself, nature is a top recycler, but if you want to help it along, build a compost heap. You'll not only reduce the amount of rubbish going into landfill, but your garden will get some great free compost, too!

What you need

- *An old wooden crate*
- *"Brown-layer" items – twigs, paper, dry stems, hair*
- *"Green-layer" items – grass clippings, fruit and vegetable peelings*

1 Choose a site for your compost container. The best is on bare soil in a sunny place. Ask an adult to help you build a simple box out of scrap wood if you don't have a box or crate large enough to hand.

Keep a 50/50 mix of "green" to "brown" items

2 Start off your heap by adding dry "brown" layers – shredded newspaper or dry straw is ideal. Add a layer of "green" items on top. Alternate the layers so you have half green and half brown.

3 Don't add cooked food, fish, dairy, or meat products– they will attract mice. Turn your heap with garden fork every few weeks. After a year, your compost should be ready for use.

356 How hot is your heap?

20 MINS

You can check that your compost heap is working by taking its temperature. Insert a long thermometer into the centre of the heap. If it reads 40–50°C (104–122°F), then your heap is breaking down at the correct rate.

Look for 40–50°C

357 Make a twig vase

30 MINS

Transform a plastic pot and some sticks into this artistic vase. Add colourful twine and an evergreen sprig, then fill it with flowers for a woodland gift.

What you need

- Plastic yogurt pot
- Thick black card
- Secateurs
- Double-sided tape
- Twine
- Twigs
- Glue
- Scissors
- Rubber band

1 Cut a piece of card long and wide enough to wrap around the pot, covering it nearly to the top. Fix it in place with the tape.

2 Ask an adult to help you cut the twigs slightly taller than the pot. Stick them around the sides with glue. Use a rubber band to hold them in place.

3 Once the glue dries, tie some raffia or coloured twine around your vase and fix it with a bow. Add a sprig of evergreen for decoration.

358 Make a shell plant pot

15 MINS

Put a plant, still in its own container, inside a larger clear plastic plant pot. Fill between the two pots with seashells so that the inner pot can't be seen.

359 Make a leaf-stencil bag

45 MINS

What you need
• Leaves • Stencil paper • Pen • Craft knife • Plate • Fabric paint • Cloth bag • Greaseproof paper • Sponges

The natural world contains many beautiful designs. Why not try stencilling one of them onto a cloth bag? Leaves work particularly well for this project, and you can use more than one shape, if you like.

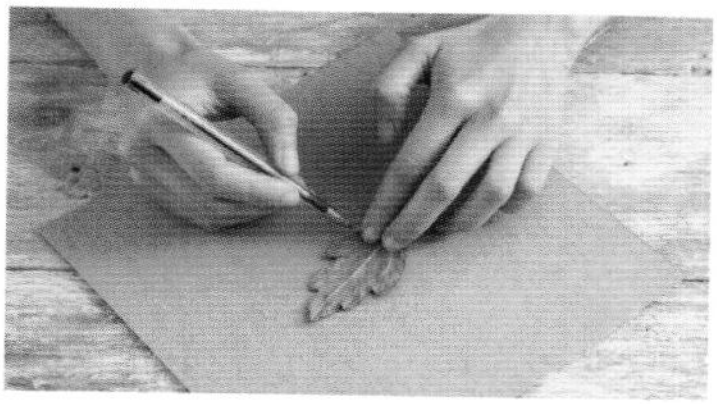

1 Trace around your chosen leaf on a piece of stencil paper. Ask an adult to help you cut out the shape with the knife.

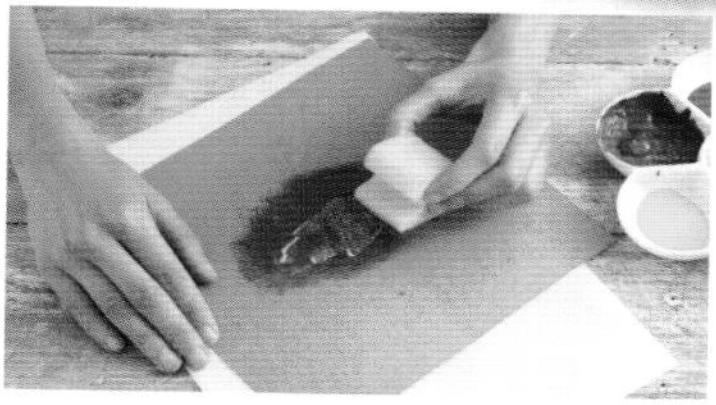

2 Cut sponges into 2–3 pieces. Put fabric paint on the plate. Dip a sponge piece into the paint and stencil it on paper to practice.

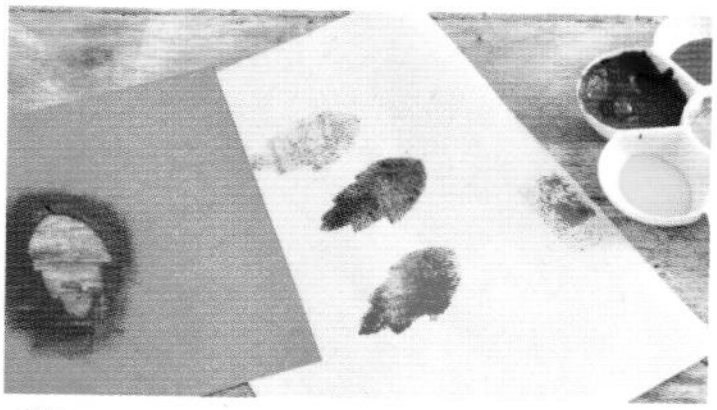

3 When you're ready, slip a piece of greaseproof paper inside the bag to stop the paint bleeding through, then sponge your stencils onto the bag.

360 Make leaf prints

20 MINS

Use leaves as stamps to make cards, book covers, or wrapping paper. Brush a layer of paint over a leaf surface, press it down on paper and smooth with your hand before lifting it off.

361 See sunspots

20 MINS

To us, the Sun looks like a large, yellow disc in the sky. Occasionally, dark sunspots appear on its face. You should never look at the Sun directly, so try this safe way to view them.

What you need

- *Two large pieces of heavy card*
- *Binoculars*
- *Paper*
- *Sticky tape*
- *Pencil*
- *Scissors*

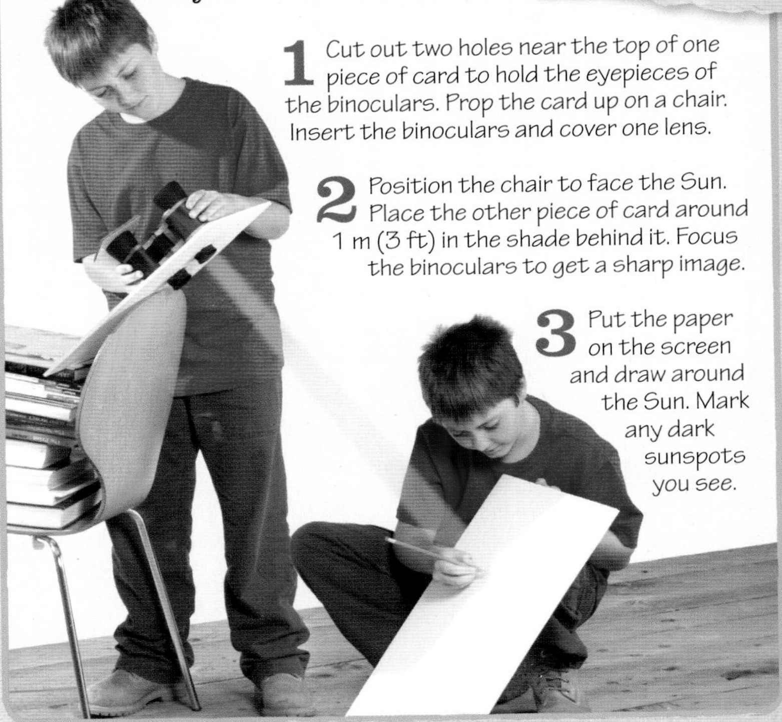

1 Cut out two holes near the top of one piece of card to hold the eyepieces of the binoculars. Prop the card up on a chair. Insert the binoculars and cover one lens.

2 Position the chair to face the Sun. Place the other piece of card around 1 m (3 ft) in the shade behind it. Focus the binoculars to get a sharp image.

3 Put the paper on the screen and draw around the Sun. Mark any dark sunspots you see.

362 View an eclipse

15 MINS

You can use the same sunspot technique to view an eclipse, which happens when the Moon passes in front of the Sun. Although eclipses are rare, they are always talked about, so listen out for one near you.

Moon passing across the Sun

363 Watch a newt grow

10 WKS

What you need
- *Access to a pond that has newts in it*

If you're lucky enough to have a nearby pond and spot a tadpole with a "frill" behind its head, it's a recently hatched newt. Why not monitor the pond and watch one of these fascinating amphibians grow up?

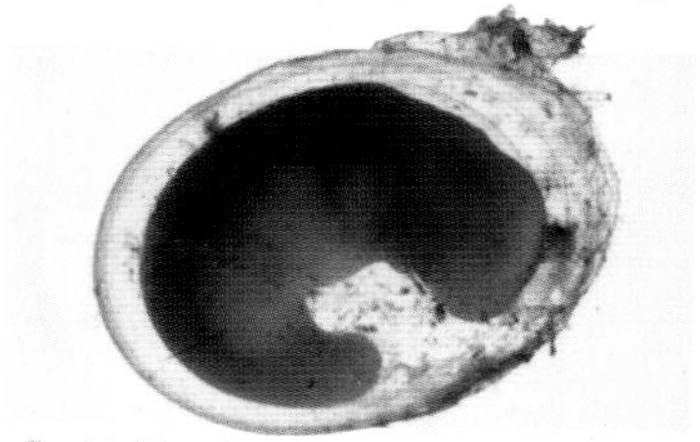

1 Unlike frogspawn, newt eggs are laid individually. Look for a single egg wrapped up in a submerged leaf.

2 A newly hatched newt eats its yolk sac, then feeds on tiny plankton. The feathery bits on either side of its head are gills.

3 After a few weeks, the minnow-like newtlet grows legs and begins to look like its parents. It can leave the water about 10 weeks after hatching.

364 Listen to frogs

15 MINS

If you're outdoors in spring or summer and there's water close by, listen to see if you can hear frogs calling. Some make a deep, throaty croak, while others, such as tree frogs, sound almost like a cricket.

Expanded vocal sac makes sounds louder

365 Play bird bingo

30 MINS

The next time you have some friends over, why not challenge them to a game of bird bingo? Set up the playing cards in advance, then go outside, watch some birds, and see who's the first to get a complete line.

What you need
- Paper
- Ruler
- Scissors
- Glue
- Pen or pencil
- Pictures of bird behaviour

1 Make playing cards with nine squares on each. Use the internet to find images of birds doing different things.

2 Print off the pictures, cut them out, and glue one in each square. Use a different order for each card.

3 Write in each behaviour below its matching picture, to make sure everyone knows what to look for.

4 Give all players a card and a pencil. Go outside and watch for behaviour. The winner is the first to cross off a line – or to tick off everything on the card.

Is it a leap year?

A year with 366 days in it is called a leap year. We need to add an extra day every four years to keep the calendar in check with the time it takes Earth to circle around the Sun. Leap years are associated with frogs so why not try one of the froggy activities in this book to mark the 366th day of the year, or have a game of leapfrog!

Index

The numbers given refer to the activity number

Acknowledgments

Dorling Kindersley would like to thank the following for their assistance in producing this book: Alison Gardner for props; Anna Hall, Charlie Noon, Anna Reinbold, Ina Stradins, Duncan Turner, and Francis Wong for design assistance; Karen Shooter and Jemima Dunne for assistance with photoshoots; Claire Bowers, Claire Cordier, Laura Evans, Lee Thompson, Romaine Werblow, and Rob Nunn for archive and picture research; Adam Stoneham for preproduction assistance; Vanessa Davies, Ria Osborne, and Howard Shooter for photography; Julie Dent for shoot location; and Izzie and Polly Alexander, Oliver Ansell, Olivia Banks, Ben and William Bristow, Alfie Chan, Kit Davies, Jesse and Alex Dent, Finlay Horastead, Isabella Linnane, Anjana Nair, Christine Ni, Erin and Samuel Regan, Kaiya Shang, Chloe, Oliver, and Luke Shooter, Henry and Oliver Tompsett, Ruby Vincent, Jorja and Mia Walsh for modeling. Also, from the Delhi office, Nand Kishore Acharya for DTP assistance, and Sumedha Chopra for compiling picture credits. The publisher would like to thank Claire Thomas at the RSPB for reviewing all the pages.

The publisher would like to thank the following for their kind permission to reproduce their photographs:

(Key: a-above; b-below/bottom; c-centre; f-far; l-left; r-right; t-top)

123RF.com: Marilyn Barbone 82cr, Chris Brignell 82cl, 82br, Sergey Galushko 23br, paulrommer 175bc, Darya Petrenko 101bl, Yann Poirier 82tl; **Alamy Images:** Juniors Bildarchiv / F314 197crb, Stephen Chung 156br, Simon Colmer 187cl, Paul Gapper 125b, Hemis 113br, Phototake Inc. 77bl, Photoshot 197clb (Soldier beetle), 197cb, Antje Schulte - Spiders and Co. 69br, Tony Watson 66bl; **Corbis:** Marilyn Angel Wynn / Nativestock Pictures 110br, Daniel Attia 144bl, Ed Darack / Science Faction 158br, Warren Faidley 65br, Ingolf Hatz 82tr, Radius Images 158cl, Morgan Petroski / Albuquerque Journal 186br, Visuals Unlimited 111br; **Dorling Kindersley:** Batsford Garden Centre and Arboretum 12-13 (Background also for 20-21,28-29,36-37,44-45,52-53,60-61,68-69,76-77,84-85,92-93, 100-101,108-109,116-117,124-125,132-133,140-141,148-149,156-157, 164-165,172-173,180-181,), Lucy Claxton 7br, Jerry Young / Jerry Young 197clb, Thomas Marent / Thomas Marent 25cl, Natural History Museum, London 17cb, 32crb, 32bc, 109br, 197tl, 197tl (Red Admiral), RHS Hampton Court Flower Show 2012 20tr, Rough Guides 17br, 120b, 128bl, 177 (Grass Background fro step 1,2,3.), Jerry Young 136br; **Dreamstime.com:** Ajafoto 52bl, Patrick Allen 131bl, Angelamaria 129b, Deosum 99br, Dule964 6-7 (Background also for 14-15,22-23,30-31,38-39,46-47,54-55, 62-63,70-71,78-79,86-87,94-95,102-103,110-111,118-119,126-127, 134-135,142-143,150-151,158-159,166-167,174-175,182-183), Sonya Etchison 147bl, Eric Isselee 199c, Isselee 197bc, Kai Koehler 139bl, Robyn Mackenzie 6 (Paper on all spreads), Mikelane45 51br, Juriah Mosin 123br, Nomadimages 63cl, Mohamed Osama 25, Prentiss40 51tl, Rachwal 188cl, Sergei Razvodovskij 6-7 (Background also on 10-11,14-15,18-19,22-23, 26-27,30-31,34-35,38-39,42-43,46-47,50-51,54-55,58-59,62-63,66-67, 70-71,74-75,78-79,82-83,86-87,90-91,94-95,98-99,102-103,106-107, 110-111,114-115,118-119,122-123,126-127,130-131,134-135,138-139, 142-143,146-147,150-151,154-155,158-159,162-163,166-167,170-171, 174-175,178-179,182-183,186-187), Alfio Scisetti 83br, Srekap 127bl, Val Thoermer 173bl, Topaz777 132bl, Witr 187cra; **FLPA:** Robert Canis 32cb, Steve Young 140cla; **Fotolia:** Jacek Chabraszewski 28bl, Thomas Dobner / Dual Aspect 180br, Maksym Dykha 97br, Eric Isselée 197clb (backswimmers); **Galaxy Picture Library:** Robin Scagel 158cla; **Getty Images:** Glowimages 87c, Kick Images / iStock Exclusive 63 (wood), 74cla, 74cra, 82tl (wood background), 94cla, 94cra, 94cl, JGI / Jamie Grill / Blend Images 164br, Charles Krebs / The Image Bank 197cl, Digital Vision / Ricky John Molloy 153cra, 153cl; **Nature Picture Library:** Adrian Davies 32br (Wild cat droppings); **naturepl.com:** Adrian Davies 32br, Alex Hyde 197tc, Rolf Nussbaumer 197c; **Pearson Asset Library:** Studio 8 135cla, 135cra, 135cl, Gareth Boden 87cr, MindStudio. 87cl, Tudor Photography 87cb, 181br, Coleman Yuen 63crb, 188c; **rspb-images.com:** Chris Gomersall 88br; **Science Photo Library:** Luke Dodd 76cla, European Southern Observatory 173cb, Thomas Heaton 94br, John Sanford 76cra, 76cl, 76cr, Barbara Strnadova 38br, 197cra

For further information see: **www.dkimages.com**

Stickers

When you finish each of the activities in this book, give yourself a star. Why not use the animal stickers to decorate a nature journal or sketchbook?